Routledge Revivals

The Growth of Fascism in Great Britain

First published in 1935, *The Growth of Fascism in Great Britain* discusses how the tendencies which have produced fascism on the European continent are by no means absent in England. The growth of fascism in England's 'green and pleasant land' is not only to be gauged by the size of the British Union of Fascists. Sir Oswald Mosley's movement follows the German and Italian models, but the economic, political, and psychological conditions of Great Britain show that the holders of power here have no immediate need of the continental method. Our conditions have dictated different tactics: it is in such measures as the Trade Disputes Act, the Means Test, the Sedition Bill, that we find the evidence of the growing attempt to achieve the substance if not the uniform of Fascism. Until it is marshalled as ably as it is here, even the serious citizen will find it difficult to form a true picture of the accumulation of this evidence. This book will cause to think all those, of whatever political creed, who love liberty.

Mr. Rudlin then proceeds to discuss the essential questions of the future: will British conditions in the end demand open Fascism? In what circumstances are we to expect the dropping of Mr. Baldwin and the taking aboard of more glamorous pilots? With an introduction by Harold J. Laski, this is an important historical document for students of British history.

The Growth of Fascism in Great Britain

W. A. Rudlin

First published in 1935
by George Allen & Unwin Ltd.

This edition first published in 2024 by Routledge
4 Park Square, Milton Park, Abingdon, Oxon, OX14 4RN

and by Routledge
605 Third Avenue, New York, NY 10017

Routledge is an imprint of the Taylor & Francis Group, an informa business

© W. A. Rudlin, 1935

All rights reserved. No part of this book may be reprinted or reproduced or utilised in any form or by any electronic, mechanical, or other means, now known or hereafter invented, including photocopying and recording, or in any information storage or retrieval system, without permission in writing from the publishers.

Publisher's Note
The publisher has gone to great lengths to ensure the quality of this reprint but points out that some imperfections in the original copies may be apparent.

Disclaimer
The publisher has made every effort to trace copyright holders and welcomes correspondence from those they have been unable to contact.

A Library of Congress record exists under LCCN: 35024316

ISBN: 978-1-032-67679-1 (hbk)
ISBN: 978-1-032-67681-4 (ebk)
ISBN: 978-1-032-67680-7 (pbk)

Book DOI 10.4324/9781032676814

W. A. RUDLIN

THE GROWTH OF FASCISM IN GREAT BRITAIN

Introduction by
HAROLD J. LASKI

LONDON
George Allen & Unwin Ltd
MUSEUM STREET

FIRST PUBLISHED IN 1935

All rights reserved
PRINTED IN GREAT BRITAIN BY
UNWIN BROTHERS LTD., WOKING

INTRODUCTION

MR. RUDLIN'S little book will have amply served its purpose if it induces the reader to realize that the tendencies which have produced fascism on the European continent are by no means absent in this country. Here, as elsewhere, capitalism in distress does not find democracy an easy yoke-fellow; and it will need something more than facile generalizations to enable us to escape the fate which has overtaken Italy and Germany and Austria.

Mr. Rudlin is concerned with diagnosis and not with cure. He points out that we are doing many of the things characteristic of those governments which have frankly abandoned the criteria and methods of democracy. It is significant that we have seriously limited the right to strike. It is significant that we have, by the Incitement to Disaffection Act, placed further limitations upon freedom of speech. It is significant that we are remodelling the police force on militarist lines. It is significant, also, that the National Government, while subsidizing industry and agriculture right and left, has shown no care for the protection of wage-standards, and has arrested (most notably in education) the development of social reform. The unhappy marriage of capitalism and democracy was made possible by the policy of continuous material concessions to the multitude. If this policy of concessions is to cease when capitalism is in distress, the historic purpose of universal suffrage seems to be frustrated *ab initio*. For universal suffrage has no point if it cannot use the power of the state to redress the balance of inequality which is inherent in the capitalist system.

And it is notable, as Mr. Rudlin points out, that the greater the difficulties capitalism encounters the less favourable is its attitude to democratic government. Of the two major parties in Great Britain to-day, it is significant that the Labour party alone pins its faith to the democratic idea. There are many conservatives prepared to see a House of Lords which can permanently frustrate the victory of socialism at the polls; there are even some who have announced that they would welcome the revival of the obsolete prerogatives of the monarchy rather than acquiesce in its consequences. This, after all, is the temper of fascism. It is the attitude which refuses to accept the freely rendered verdict of the electorate if this is unfavourable to its interests. Those who, like Mr. Runciman, urge their friends to follow up a socialist victory by a run on the banks, are driving opinion to exactly that temper in which the hope of rational compromise is lost.

No doubt if the problem came to an issue in this country, we should wear our fascism with a difference. No doubt the long tradition of constitutionalism would make Hitlerite methods far less acceptable than they have proved in Germany. But I think the reader of Mr. Rudlin's pages will do well to reflect while there is still time. Unless he understands the gravity of the issue, he will find himself surprised by crisis not less easily than his continental neighbours. We are no longer free from the implications of the world market. We can no longer fashion our history without regard to the processes in which we are so deeply involved. The class-structure of our society leads, in the absence of a militant vigilance, to the same fate as has overtaken other peoples. Unless we remember that, as Pericles said, the secret of liberty is courage, we may realize our position only after the battle is lost. If Mr. Rudlin's book warns us to heed where we are going, it will not have been written in vain.

HAROLD J. LASKI

CONTENTS

Introduction
by HAROLD J. LASKI
PAGE 7

Chapter One
The End of Expansion
PAGE 13

Chapter Two
Fascist Theory and Capitalist Practice
PAGE 28

Chapter Three
The Decline of British Capitalism
PAGE 39

Chapter Four
The New Economic Policy
PAGE 48

Chapter Five
The Withdrawal of British Democracy
PAGE 74

Chapter Six
Reaction—The Next Stage
PAGE 104

Index
PAGE 137

THE GROWTH OF FASCISM IN GREAT BRITAIN

I

THE END OF EXPANSION

GREAT BRITAIN has hitherto escaped the rigours of fascism in its classic form. We have no Dictator, and such comparisons as are made between Mosley and his continental models are subject to serious—or humorous—reservations. And whether the fascists of Britain have or have not ceased to be, in Sir Oswald's phrase, "black-shirted buffoons, making a cheap imitation of ice-cream sellers,"[1] they have, as yet, not acquired those facilities for widespread terrorism without which no Fascist party is fully equipped.

Such considerations as these will be, to many people, a source of great satisfaction. As aids to speculation about the political future of Britain they are not, however, of great value. For while it is pleasant to reflect that Mosley is not Hitler or Mussolini, it is also as well to remember that there was once no Führer or Duce, but only an Austrian house-painter, humbly making bookshelves for the party's first headquarters, and an Italian socialist

[1] At a meeting in 1927 at Cambridge which was broken up by "several hundred undergraduates, carrying Union Jacks and fascist flags." See *Who Backs Mosley?* published by the Labour Research Department.

with pacifist tendencies and a notable moustache. And if it seems a far cry from the imitative buffoonery of Olympia and Hyde Park to a fascist Britain, it is again well to remember that the Ludendorff–Hitler *putch* of 1923 was an ignominious failure.

Turning from the uniform to the substance of fascism, there is even less reason for satisfaction. In Britain, it is true, parliamentary government has not been abandoned, nor has it become impossible for the British working man to attempt to safeguard his interests. We have not suffered that complete destruction of every democratic principle which has followed upon the victory of fascism in Italy, Germany, and Austria. Following upon the victory of the National Government in Britain, we have, however, seen an increasingly marked tendency to remove the governmental process from the sphere of parliamentary control, to restrict the opportunities of free speech and free assembly, to prosecute for political offences, and to place upon the Statute Book such measures as the Unemployment Act and the Sedition Act.

This is not, of course, to suggest that the National Government is a fascist dictatorship, or that, in Britain, the full purposes of fascism have been achieved. What is suggested is that there is a resemblance, in kind if not in degree, between continental achievements and those of the National Government; a resemblance sufficiently close to prompt an inquiry into the existence, in a democratic Britain, of fascist tendencies. Such an enquiry must follow two main lines: it is necessary to know, first, the economic, political, and social conditions in which fascism develops, and, second, the extent to

THE END OF EXPANSION 15

which such conditions exist or are likely to exist in Britain.

A very slight acquaintance with the post-war history of Europe is sufficient to show the importance of economic factors in the rise of fascism. Hitler came to power—with an overwhelming superiority of 1·7 per cent of the votes cast—on the promise of economic recovery no less than on that of national rebirth. It was the world crisis and the Bruening Hunger Decrees which by the autumn of 1931 had increased eightfold the votes of the party which, four years earlier, had been declining rapidly, notwithstanding all its reliance on youth, racial purity, the old tribal gods, and a bottomless purse. The heady delights of a Risorgimento lubricated with castor-oil were undoubtedly attractive to a younger generation more than a little ashamed of Caporetto. But it was the promise of industrial peace and the prospect of a colonial empire finer than that for which Orlando wept at Versailles that brought the business man hurrying to drop his *lire* in the party chest.

Fascism arises out of, though not solely because of, economic distress. It does not, however, arise out of the economic distress of those communities which have not yet tried the system of private ownership of the means of production. Nor does it arise in those communities where private ownership has, after trial, been abolished. Only in the economic distress of capitalist societies does fascism find a suitable breeding-ground. For only in capitalist societies does economic distress occur in the midst of economic plenty.

The essence of capitalism is the private ownership of the means of production, and, as the result of such ownership, a stream of free income in the form of interest, profit, rent, and royalties. That income is expended partly in ordinary—or extraordinary—living, partly in reinvestment in further means of production which in turn provide new income for reinvestment. Capitalism is, therefore, a method by which the means of production can be profitably accumulated, and the problems of production successfully solved.

It relies for its success, however, upon the maintenance of an equilibrium between production and consumption. The circular process which begins and ends with investment must provide not only durable capital goods but also purchasing power with which may be bought the consumable products of durable goods. The rhythm of that process, the equilibrium of the whole "system," depends upon cumulative investment in more and more durable goods which distributes an increasing flow of purchasing power with which to make possible the sale of ever greater supplies of consumers' goods—at a profit to be reinvested. But without an increase or extension of purchasing power proportionate to an increasing volume of production, equilibrium is upset and the urge to reinvestment checked by the prospect of unprofitable sales. It becomes no longer possible to utilize the new developments of technique and productive power, since existing plant is already producing a surplus fatal to the realization of profits. On the one hand stocks and productive capacity accumulate, on the other hand poverty and unemployment.

That inability to utilize the new developments of technique and productive power is one of the most obvious characteristics of modern capitalism. A society based upon private ownership and profit making has arrived at a point from which it can make no further productive advance within the limits of property relations. For with enormous increases in production and far more enormous increases in productive power has come world crisis, vast and unsaleable stocks of goods, productive stagnation, and unemployment for thirty million people. If any further productive advance is to be made, or even if the ground won in the past is to be maintained, some means must be found of providing new effective demand. The history of capitalism has in fact been in large part the record of constant search for fresh purchasing power, for fresh regions to "develop." Whatever its successes in the past, however, it is unlikely that further search will yield much of value. The greater part of the world and its markets were already divided up amongst monopolist empires in 1914, and the redivision at Versailles left—China apart—little possibility of further expansion. There are virtually no new regions to open up, a large potential market has turned its back on the capitalist world and, so far from there being new worlds to conquer, the old one has begun to contract.

One alternative to the discovery of new sources of purchasing power would seem to be the development of the old. But whatever its attractions in theory or in the United States, such a policy cannot over a long period be harmonized with the essential purposes of a capitalist economy, whether of the "classic," or present-day monopolist type. For to increase the purchasing power of a market which cannot absorb the output of a vast productive mechanism is equivalent to raising costs of production, for in order that demand be made more "effective" industry must pay higher wages, or recipients of free income must pay in higher taxes for state subsidies to consumers. Either method is a deterrent to profitable investment and can result only in the further lowering of productive activity. Another alternative would seem to be to allow capitalism to pursue its "normal" course, by which is meant the course it was wont to follow in its classic days. There was a time when any marked disequilibrium, due to an excess of supply over demand, would have driven prices down and the less efficient producers to the wall. The disappearance of the latter was the harsh but effective means whereby capitalism was able to restore equilibrium whenever, in the absence of new markets abroad, the recipients of free income were so unwise as to invest for home consumption. We are, however, no longer in the classic days of capitalism. The post-war world has become more and more a world of monopoly capitalism, and the student of economics who is interested in understanding the present rather than in reincarnating the past will proceed from "equilibrium analysis" to the theory of monopoly price. He will note the passing, even in pre-war days, of free trade and the free market regulation of demand and supply. He will note the instability of a post-war capitalism, "restored" for a short period with American subsidies, and then brought down in crisis by the tariffs, quotas, subsidies, reparations, and debts of all those swarming economic nationalisms that have blessed the union of the state and Big Business. He will proceed to the study of great monopolies which sought, for the most part successfully, to meet world depression by maintaining monopoly prices above the general price level.[1] And he may conclude that modern capitalism has reached the stage where it can neither be purged by regular depressions such as served to correct the irregularities of its younger days, nor won back to health by a steady diet of fresh markets.

The old remedies are unavailable or unavailing. What, then, can capitalism do? It can do what in large measure it has already done: it can prevent the further development of productive capacity, destroy wealth, restrict production, resign itself to permanent large-scale unemployment, turn its back on internationalism of every kind, and take steps to silence the advocates of alternative systems. Recognizing that the period of expansion is at an end and that productive advance is only possible at the expense of private profit, capitalism makes its inevitable choice. A system based upon private ownership of the means of production cannot permit anything which menaces the sanctity of free income. It must, therefore, if it is to maintain itself, sacrifice productivity and proceed to the organization of decline.

During five years of crisis, organized decline has become an integral part of the economic process. The slaughtering of sows in farrow, the burning of cattle and

[1] From the first half of 1929 to 1933 the prices of cartellized goods in Germany fell 20 per cent. Non-cartellized goods in the same period fell 55 per cent.—*World Production*, League of Nations, p. 109.

coffee, the ploughing up or abandoning of millions of acres of cotton, wheat, and tobacco, the dismantling of machinery and shipyards—all such practices have passed from the realm of the fantastic to that of the commonplace. Capitalist society no longer questions the wisdom of government organization of restriction and destruction. It is slowly becoming acclimatized to the atmosphere of decay.

As the German people are beginning to realize, however, the process of acclimatization will take time. The possibilities of destruction are vast and have by no means been exhausted. In sacrificing productivity to profits it is not enough to stop the machine; while the machine remains it is a constant menace, capable always, since production is "private" and enterprise "individual," of producing too much wealth. In order to prevent the recurrence of such a disaster something must be done to check the use of machinery and the advance of invention. From the attack on productivity we pass logically to the attack on the idea of machinery in particular and science in general. Politicians like M. Joseph Caillaux and Lord Eustace Percy, when faced with the problems of unemployment and a flow of wealth too great to be absorbed, have decided that the machine has great dangers for humanity, and that man must free himself from the tyranny of inventions which may suddenly augment his powers to produce. If, as with M. Caillaux, the approach to politics is financial, the solution is state restriction of invention. If, as with Lord Eustace Percy, the approach is mystical, the solution offered is a return to the simple crafts of the pre-machine age.

Over a wide field capitalist society has begun to reject a nineteenth-century ideology which could proudly boast of gradual solution of the problems of production. Having reached the limits of its advance it is making the dispositions necessary for orderly retreat. In an army which has begun the long march back, which has begun to relinquish ground previously conquered, the spirit of advance has no place. It is frowned upon as being dangerous since it may give rise to criticism of the high command. Defeat implies, in short, the abandonment of any idea of progress, economic or otherwise, which is incompatible with the passive and orderly acceptance of defeat. A liberal science, a belief in the power of reason, a liberal social development—these had their place in the period of capitalist expansion. But with the passing of that spacious age has come the revolt against its ideology. Science is denied, not merely by its traditional opponents, but by its own leaders, who hasten to proclaim its humility in the presence of religion and to demonstrate, for popular instruction, its impotence in the face of the utter mysteriousness of the universe.

With the desertion of liberal science there takes place, and for the same reason, the desertion of liberal politics. The belief in the inevitability of political and social progress is dying with the belief in the inevitability of scientific progress. Political democracy becomes popular as the instrument by which a rising middle class is able to emancipate itself from the restrictions of aristocratic privilege. It remains popular while a dominant bourgeoisie can afford in the days of expansion to grant social reforms and economic concessions. But when expansion ends and decline begins, capitalism finds it necessary not only to discontinue the provision of concessions, but also to cut down and withdraw those already made. And in order to carry out such a policy with expedition and despatch, it must free itself from the encumbrances of a democratic system of government which permits popular demands for reforms and opposition to their withdrawal. A society which has admitted the expediency but not the principle of concessions has no place, in a period of decline, for democratic institutions which formerly allowed the working class to demand a share in expansion and through which it can now demand the reform or replacement of a system no longer able to achieve productive advance. If capitalism is to survive it can contemplate no alternative to economic reaction. Parliamentary debate, constitutional procedure, all democratic forms which are linked with the drive towards economic equality, become therefore both superfluous and dangerous. A movement arises to change them, or where decline is most marked, to replace them with coercive machinery guaranteed to operate only in reverse gear.

With these internal problems of capitalist society there must be reckoned certain external problems, which, as Germany has discovered, are not so easily solved. In its international aspect capitalism has developed into an increasingly acute struggle between imperialist powers for the world market. A system which once based itself upon free competition and free trade has long been forced to deny that basis by its introduction of the power of the state into the sphere of economic conflict. Once a competitor enters the world market he cannot, if he is to survive, dispense with the assistance and protection of his government. So the competition for foreign markets, as it became more and more severe, made of the world of states an uneasy gathering of hostile imperialisms, each heavily armed for the safeguarding of its possessions, and for their extension, either by the diplomatic force of power and prestige which arms afford, or by direct annexation. As Joseph Chamberlain said: "The Empire is commerce . . . it was created by commerce, it is founded on commerce and it would not exist a day without commerce. . . . For these reasons, among others, I would never lose the hold which we now have over our great Indian dependency—by far the greatest and most valuable of all customers we have or ever shall have in this country. For the same reasons I approve of the continued occupation of Egypt . . . and lastly it is for the same reasons that I hold that our Navy should be strengthened until its supremacy is so assured that we cannot be shaken in any of the possessions which we hold, or may hold hereafter."[1]

The central fact of the pre-war international world was the existence of a number of imperialist blocs each of which clung jealously to its sovereignty in order to ensure its economic survival. In such conditions no surrender of sovereignty was possible, no hope of common world interest could triumph over the fear and suspicion of rival "national" interests.

Moreover, in the post-war period of decline the movement towards closed monopolist empires, which is imperialism, has been enormously accelerated. In the

[1] *Foreign and Colonial Speeches*, p. 101.

background of the struggle for closed markets the idea of a World Economic Conference was conceived, a conference which should have as its purpose the rehabilitation of an economy that can produce wealth but cannot distribute it. And it was in that background that the Conference was destined to failure. For there exists no unitary world capitalism capable of adopting the recommendations of a Loveday or a Salter. There exists only a world of capitalisms in a conflict which cannot be solved in capitalist terms, and which must therefore be continued, however clearly the experts may demonstrate the cost, in restricted trade and lowered standards of life.

The Conference failed and immediately there began an intensification of economic conflict, a fresh turning inwards of economic policies. The period following has seen the employment of virtually every instrument of economic warfare in the effort to conquer the foreign market. Every Power, in order to retain or increase its share of the market, has been forced to take up the weapons of subsidy and wage reductions and currency manipulation. And since entry into the foreign market has come to depend upon the maintenance of a closed home market, another group of weapons must be used. Tariffs, quotas, surtaxes, import prohibitions—all such instruments in restraint of trade are brought into operation to strengthen the internal organization of monopoly in order that the struggle may go on for closed markets, privileged areas of exploitation, and control of sources of raw material.

More politely, resort is had to "planning" and "national

THE END OF EXPANSION 25

self-sufficiency." It will, however, need more than the spate of propaganda for planning that has followed, since the Conference went home, to disguise the fact that there can be no scientifically planned or regulated economy within a system founded upon private ownership for private profit. For the one implies some form of social ownership with control directed to social ends—an implication which the other knows to be at odds with its basic principles. National self-sufficiency is merely the name given to the domestic exigencies of foreign conflict. It means the production at home of what can be more cheaply produced abroad.[1]

Each competing unit relies ultimately upon military power to guard its privileged areas and annexed territory, raw material supplies, and closed colonial markets. The more trade becomes a function of the limits of "empire," the more armaments are needed to guard or extend those limits. But the "foreigner" must have greater armaments too, as any pedlar of arms, from Zaharoff down, will testify, for he must prepare against, if not for, encroachment. And when all the places in the sun have been "occupied" or "pacified" or "influenced" and capitalist decline has set in with its intensification of economic warfare, the need for encroachment on the one hand and defence on the other becomes more and more urgent. Liberalism will have erected a "Peace System," but it will have been overshadowed by a Power system intent

[1] The Berlin correspondent of the Associated Press reported on October 5, 1934: "How far Germany is prepared to go in her desperate fight for self-sufficiency was disclosed to-day in a government order for peat and coal operators to produce petrol even though it costs four times the world price."

on upholding a Treaty which was itself a redistribution of spoils. A League of Nations will have applied itself with vigour and enthusiasm to the preservation of peace. Its supporters, as each tidy little plan seems inadequate, will move nimbly and without self-questioning from the "sanctions" of Article 16 to an International Army and thence to an International Air Police Force. When war seems remote—when, for example, Great Britain shows signs of joining with the U.S.A. in discouraging Japanese adventures—they will talk of the Collective System. But when at a Naval Conference Mr. MacDonald estranges the U.S.A. by giving Japan *carte blanche* to disturb the peace of the northern half of the Pacific, they will discuss, with undiminished fervour the *need* for a Collective System. They will conduct research and propaganda on a vast scale, but always on the understanding that war prevention is a business to be undertaken without regard to the major causes of war. They will continue to be blind to the tendency of capitalism to engender wars out of economic rivalry, even after the coming of world depression has coincided with "revival" in the armament industry, and the final flouting of the sham "collective security." They will see nothing significant, even in such a creed as that of Baron Seinosuké Go, president of the Japanese Chamber of Commerce and Industry, and of the Japanese Economic League: "There are two ways of getting the better of over-production in Japan. One is to conquer foreign markets. The other is to turn producers into consumers. But the second way is impracticable. The only remaining way, therefore, is territorial expansion. The Manchurian question is important in this connection. . . . The best way of defeating increasingly acute competition is to make oneself safe by acquiring markets and territory of one's own. It is in this that the danger of war lies."[1]

Even if the Comité des Forges, the Bank of Paris, the German Supreme Economic Council, the Federation of British Industries, and every other society for the propagation of monopoly were to make as frank a delineation of realities as that of the Japanese Chamber, it is doubtful whether the advocates of the "Collective Security Plan" would acknowledge the relation between profits and war. They would probably continue to demonstrate, with superb logic, that because war has been the recourse of every known form of government it cannot be inherent in the capitalist system.

[1] See "Economic Imperialism" in *New Statesman and Nation*, October 27, 1934.

II

FASCIST THEORY AND CAPITALIST PRACTICE

AFTER a century of political and economic progress, capitalism finds itself forced to go into reverse gear. The large-scale restriction and destruction of wealth and productive capacity, the revolt against the machine, the abandonment of international trade, the acceptance of large-scale unemployment as a permanent characteristic of the system, the movement away from democracy and parliamentary government—all these point to a process of decay within the capitalist order. And in those states where decline is most marked the process of decay is carried furthest, and may find its political expression in fascism.

It will find its expression in fascism when the need to organize decay has become acute and when opposition to or interference with the policies of reaction is strong enough to threaten their successful application. Opposition will come from communists, social democrats, Labour parties, and trade unions—all those who, for various reasons, take their stand against those policies of reduction of wages and withdrawal of social concessions which are inevitable for a capitalism in distress. Interference will come from democratic forms and institutions. In the period of decline there is no hope of further concessions, no possibility of another gradualist experiment, no alternative to reaction, and therefore nothing which lends itself to the democratic procedure of discussion, debate, and majority rule. Political democracy is bereft of function; no longer an adequate safety-valve for the accumulation of social discontent, it becomes, at best, a time-wasting obstruction and, at worst, a menace to the effective working out of the policies of capitalist reaction.

If the march of events towards economic crisis is not too rapid, if the challenge via democratic institutions has no great terrors for a strong capitalist government with a large majority, the tightening of the hold of private property over the state can be carried out for the most part under the mask of the usual constitutional forms. Some resort to the violent methods of Hitler and Mussolini may be necessary, but the main effect will be achieved "constitutionally" through the transformation of existing political parties, and their fusion into some kind of "National Government," by means of which a not-so-hard-pressed capitalism will be able to do all that is necessary in the way of dispensing with the "consent of the governed."

But if capitalism, as in Germany, shows signs of plunging off the long slope of depression into the abyss of crisis; if, as in Germany and Italy, democratic institutions can neither bring about socialism nor rehabilitate capitalism—if, in short, the real holders of power are faced with a desperate situation, they will need to have recourse to a desperate remedy. They will need to create or adopt a mass movement, provide it with funds, dictate its policies, ostensible and real, and name the enemies which it is to attack. Armed with such an instrument they will not be backward in applying the policies of reaction to the problems of economic crisis. Where the regular forces of the state are inadequate for the suppression of protest they can be supplemented by a private army, trained to the destruction of working-class and liberal organizations. Where democratic mechanisms become superfluous or dangerous they can be replaced by the functionless little devices of a corporate state, diligently assembled to distract the eye from the working of the despotic steamroller.

This building of a mass party is not, in the conditions of a post-war world, an unduly difficult operation. There are in every capitalist state numbers of ex-Army officers who, since the war, have found no homes for heroes, no work, or who have exchanged the responsible functions of war-time leadership for the delights of travelling salesmanship; of technicians who find their professions increasingly overcrowded as productive advance ceases; of small business men and shopkeepers who are bought out or blotted out by the development of monopoly; of farmers and peasants who cannot sell their produce to poverty-stricken urban workers; of students equipped with skill and knowledge which society needs but cannot afford; of black-coated workers trying to maintain the standards of one class on earnings less than those of the more fortunate members of the class below; small savers and investors, reared in the tradition of stable middle-class incomes and ruined by high taxes, inflation, and monopoly prices; of unemployed, those whom a socialist Prime Minister called "human scrap," who can appreciate the full significance of the phrase but not that of the author; of every kind of person suffering from the psychology of defeat, individual or national or both.

These "discontented and disillusioned elements," largely bereft of property, status, and self-respect, form the perfect audience for anyone who can promise a new supply of and sanctity for private property, who can restore individual and national self-respect by providing uniforms, bands, and comradeship; *action*, discipline, and faith in place of dissension, disorganization, and doubt.

The socialist parties—Social Democratic or Communist—have so far been unable to discover a technique for reaping this mixed harvest. The small man bears no love for a Social Democratic party whose policy, in his experience, is but a blind insistence on social services and higher wages regardless of whether industry can afford to foot the bill. Nor will anything reconcile him to the prospect of complete and final expropriation, which is, for him, the only meaning of communism. In any case the parties of the Left lack the funds with which to provide the bread and circuses necessary to convert a distressed and unstable middle element into a powerful political movement.

Nor can this element organize itself into a "third party." The Liberal programme of a prosperous middle class—social reform, democratic advance, internationalism in politics and trade—no longer has any relation to its needs. When it attempts to construct a new party platform it finds that other parties are already in possession of the best materials, and that nothing remains but some few pieces of untrimmed Douglas fir and Californian redwood.

But the hope of a third alternative springs eternal. There must be some way out which shall be neither large-scale capitalism with its monopolies and wicked financiers nor socialism with its "levelling down." There must be some way to avoid the class struggle by planning, or currency reform, or a new deal, or by hating the foreigner or the Jew or the communist. The only difficulty is to synthesize all these solutions into one party programme to which all may subscribe. There are always, however, the Strassers, the Feders, and the Mussolinis who can put together at short notice some kind of philosophy out of a socialism with reservations, a romantic nationalism and some sort of Hegelian mysticism. There is always the nucleus of a Fascist party which knows that its ultimate purpose is the maintenance of capitalism, and that the degree of financial support it obtains will depend upon its ability to build up a party which can be used as the instrument for the attack on democracy. So the little group of ex-officers and political adventurers sets out to win support by promising higher prices for the farmer and lower prices for the housewife; higher wages for the worker and the abolition of unions for the employer; the expansion of the fatherland and the abolition of interest; the safeguarding of private property and nationalization of banks, industry, and the land. The promises may be mutually contradictory—what matter, if they attract votes. The potential rank and file of Fascisti may hate Big Business as much as they hate socialism, but they will not be reminded of the fact that his trial in 1924 proved Hitler to be enjoying the financial backing of large-scale industry. They will not be told that the price of their uniforms and soup-kitchens came from the Bergbauverein Essen and the Nordwestgruppe der Essen und Stahlindustrie, nor that any strain on the purse of the Ruhr Steel Trust can be relieved by application to the Federation of German Industries.[1]

The fascist policy as advertised may be impossible of fulfilment, but those people to whom it is meant to appeal will never know it until it is too late. Revelling in the psychological relief of having found a leader who will give them a new status, a new function, and a new self-respect, the young men of the party will never stop to ask where the money is coming from. No rational argument will make headway against their will-to-believe. No weight of evidence except that of bitter experience will destroy the faith in the leader, the hope of a new society, the charity which sees in the proceeds of house-to-house collections the peaceful solution to the class war.

It is only after money and propaganda and gifted demagogy, working upon every ambition, prejudice, and superstition of a distressed middle class, have built up a powerful mass movement, that the party member begins to examine the real meaning of fascism. Then he may remember that the "fundamentals" of the party programme called for a state-guaranteed individualism, a *laissez-faire* small-scale capitalism in which trusts and trade unions would not exist. And he may find that the fascist reality is somewhat different, that corporate state and all, it means little more than the suppression of

---

[1] For detailed investigation into the financial backing of German fascism, see E. Mowrer, *Germany Puts the Clock Back*, and Ernst Henri's *Hitler over Europe*.

working-class rights and organizations, with the state keeping the ring for monopoly capital. He may remember the early promises of increased production, higher wages, higher profits, and a solution to unemployment, and reflect that after twelve years of perfecting the fascist "system", Italy has suffered as severely as any country from the world depression and more severely than most; that Italian exports and imports fell by 50 per cent in two years; that "while the cost of living with an index figure of 93·78 in 1927 has fallen in 1932 to 78·05, a difference of 15·73 per cent, individual wages have been reduced by much larger proportions";[1] that the official figure for unemployment for January 1934 was 1,158,000, exclusive of 200,000 on short time; and that the compulsory unemployment insurance—one shilling per day, for a maximum of four months—was paid in 1932 to less than 25 per cent of the unemployed.

Mussolini's advent to power came at the beginning of a short period of economic ascension. He had time, therefore, to experiment and to disguise with an occasional concession his close relationship with the large-scale industrialists who have financed his movement. In Germany, however, Hitler was in no such fortunate position; the urgencies of crisis had to be met at once without disguise and with no attempt to relate what was being done to what the party programmes had promised would be done. The economic situation demanded longer

[1] The Report of the Commercial Counsellor of the British Embassy at Rome. See *Economic Conditions in Italy*, 1933, Department of Overseas Trade Report. H.M. Stationery Office. 5s.

FASCIST THEORY AND CAPITALIST PRACTICE 35

hours, lower wages, and increased rationalization; the corporate state remained, as it had always been, a demagogic fiction. To this was added the rise in the price of staple goods and food products, the failure of the work-providing scheme, the steady worsening of the economic condition of the middle and lower classes, and the diplomatic setbacks in regard to the Polish Corridor and the claims to Austria.

These developments, while clearly at variance with the sham-socialism of earlier days, did not immediately scandalize the rank and file of fascist followers, who, surrounded by the stupefying vapours of propaganda, were prepared to accept standstill and even reaction as an essential preliminary step towards fascist "socialism." But as it became clear that reaction would not be succeeded by reform, the feeling began to develop that all was not as it should be. Farmers, tradesmen, labourers, even sections of the Brown Army, found their faith a little shaken. The demand grew for a "second revolution" in order to fulfil the pledges of the sacred Nazi programme. In other words, the usefulness of the movement to its backers began to decline. Just as social democracy in the post-war period of decline ceased to operate as an adequate safety-valve against revolution, so Nazism, when in deepening crisis it begins to discover the essential nature of fascist purposes, begins also to lose its value as an instrument for the perpetuation of capitalist power. It becomes necessary, therefore, to "reorganize" the party, in somewhat the same way as a few years before, it had become necessary to "reorganize" the Socialist and Communist parties. For, in that period, the prime need of German capitalism has remained unchanged. In the carrying out of the reactionary policies of restriction and destruction, which are imperative for a capitalism in distress, a completely free hand is essential. Fascism is one technique whereby that free hand may be obtained, whereby in states acutely menaced by crisis all opposition to capitalist "remedies" can be crushed with an expedition and despatch befitting the urgency of crisis. But, like its democratic predecessor, it is a technique which will be retained only for as long as it can command popular support—as long, that is, as the Nazi is content to give thanks for "the new spirit of the German people" and "national regeneration" and to ask for nothing more. But in the degree to which the rank and file of the movement begins to demand that psychological revival be followed by economic reform, the popular support of fascism becomes less an asset than a liability, and capitalism turns to the discovery of some new technique whereby its perpetuation may be assured.

This is the significance of the killings of June 30, 1934. So out of harmony were the Left-wing Nazis in their simple expectations and their guileless surprise at the increasing apparent dependence of Hitler upon his financial impresarios that the Führer had, for some time before the glorious thirtieth, been planning to disband his million Brownshirts. A month's vacation, without uniform or arms, to begin on July 1st, had been decided upon when von Papen's outburst, friction between the Storm Troops and the Stahlhelm and the restiveness of his backers—notably Herr Krupp von Bohlen—forced Hitler to take drastic measures. Behind him were the powerful capitalist interests whose bidding he wished to perform. To his right were the reactionary and by no means negligible remains, Junkers and bureaucrats, of the pre-war Germany. To his left were those S.A. men, Roehm, Ernst, Heines, and a number of minor lieutenants who were dissatisfied with his policy or jealous of his personal prestige or both. In this highly critical situation the unknown quantity was the Reichswehr. Exposed to the intrigues of the ambitious Schleicher, it might be used to bring the former Chanceller back to power. But under the control of General von Blomberg, always Hitler's staunch ally, it would provide that armed support which would be essential if the Leader were to pursue the only course consistent with his retention of personal power and industrial backing—the abandonment of the Right and of the Left. Hence the murder of Schleicher, to ensure the predominance of von Blomberg; the murder of Bose, the right-hand man of von Papen, as a warning to all Junkers, ex-Army officers and officials of the pre-war regime with untotalitarian leanings; the murder of Roehm, Ernst, and Heines to prevent their development of the S.A. men into a separate power in the state, and the murder of a number of minor S.A. leaders with romantic attachments to their articles of faith. The Brown Army is "reorganized," power is taken from the hands of young men zealous for reform and placed in the hands of the professional army and the carefully chosen, black-uniformed, S.S. bodyguard. It is the measure of the distress of German capitalism that it is being forced to adopt that most uncertain and dangerous of all techniques—the military dictatorship.

The latest evidence of Hitler's desertion of the movement and programme that helped him to power is contained in the report of December 6, 1934, that Gottfried Feder, who wrote most of the "unalterable" twenty-five theses of the National Socialist party, has been "placed on the retired list." Beginning as Under-Secretary in the Economics Ministry in the early days of Nazi rule, he was later placed on a shelf in the Commissariat for Suburban Land Settlement. He stands for the "economy of blood and soil," strict autarchy, rigid control of prices, production, and distribution, nationalization of the banks, and public works financed through non interest-bearing treasury notes. He was bound, therefore, to fall foul of Dr. Shacht, who has definite ideas on the subject of the devaluation of the mark, and of Thyssen, Krupp von Bohlen, and other leaders of German business, who are no less definite on the subject of a return to manorial-handicraft medieval economy. His experience is typical of what has happened to the whole German middle class. Won over by the promise of a new society, they are sent home when, having destroyed the enemy, they begin to suggest that the promises be fulfilled.

III

THE DECLINE OF BRITISH CAPITALISM

No capitalist state has been able to withstand the forces making for decline. None, therefore, has been able to dispense with the policies of retrogression and reaction upon which capitalist survival depends. Where events marched rapidly towards economic and political crisis those policies could not be carried out except by the methods of fascism. But in those countries where crisis is less severe, where the working-class challenge is weaker, where democratic political forms continue to command popular respect, where the middle element is less bewildered and distressed, politically, economically, and psychologically—in short, where the conditions of pre-fascist Italy, Germany, and Austria exist in a lesser degree—there is the less need for violence and reaction, and the less need for the specific fascist technique. Where private property is threatened but does not see itself in imminent danger of complete economic crisis and political overthrow, it will be content with a smaller degree of political reaction.

Any measures thus taken are fascist in the sense that they are taken with the object of achieving those capitalist purposes which have nowhere been more completely achieved than in the three fascist states. The country which takes such measures exhibits a tendency towards fascism, even though it may not have proceeded, in its search for a bulwark against crisis, as far as the bourgeoisie of Italy, Germany, and Austria found it necessary to go.

There is, as yet, no mass fascist movement in Great Britain, no immediate prospect of widespread terrorism, no strong tendency away from parliamentary government, and no middle class bewildered and distressed to the point of desperation. But capitalism in Great Britain, like its foreign counterparts, has for years past been moving in the direction of economic decline, and, in anticipation of the distance it will have to travel in this direction, it has begun to devote itself, under the exploratory genius of Mr. MacDonald, to the selection of those political and economic avenues of reaction down which it will be able to proceed with the smallest loss to itself and the least possible opposition from those whom it proposes to take with it. It has, in short, begun to exhibit fascist tendencies.

There were many signs, even before the Great War, that British capitalism was entering a period of decline. An individualist industrial structure, haphazardly put together for the purpose of making hay while the sun shone on world monopoly, began, in the 'nineties, to show its weaknesses in the face of French and German competition. The gold boom of the Boer War period could not entirely hide the fact that the basic industries of Britain had passed their prime. The armaments race of the immediate pre-war period came to their rescue, but by 1914 it was clear that German competition was about to triumph decisively in Africa, the Near East, and the Argentine.

For fifty years before the war Britain had been turning

more and more away from domestic industry and trade towards foreign investment and international financial services. With the subordination of wages to profits a starved home market could not absorb the output which an ever-increasing productivity and capital accumulation made possible. The result was the large-scale export of British capital, increasing dependence upon foreign enterprise rather than upon home industry and the home market, with, consequently, increasing unemployment, further impoverishment of the home market. Only one-fifth of the money raised in the City between 1908 and 1913 was used for domestic purposes: the rest went abroad to develop foreign rivals to British industry.

The Bolshevik revolution deprived British ownership of its large share in Russian industry. Japan seized the opportunity of the war to enter into intensive competition with Britain in the Eastern markets, particularly in the textile trades. India, financed largely by British capital, developed its own textile industry. The decline in armament expenditure after 1919, the loss of the valuable German market, and the enormously swollen National Debt completed a set of economic conditions the immediate reflection of which was, in 1921, an acute depression and a million unemployed.

Since the war the decline has continued. As early as the autumn of 1920 it was apparent that the position of British industry in the post-war world was greatly inferior to the position it had occupied in 1913. The war had eaten up £650,000,000 of British investments in the U.S.A. and a further £100,000,000 of foreign investment elsewhere. The United States, freed from external debt, began the economic penetration of areas—Canada, Mexico, the Argentine, Brazil, Chile, and Bolivia—which had hitherto been regarded as primarily British preserves. With the restoration of the Gold Standard competition from foreign rivals became more acute; prices fell, wages were reduced, and unemployment increased. The coal crisis of 1926 was not an isolated disaster; it merely marked an especially low point in a British depression, which was made even worse as time went on by growing American and German competition and by Chinese and Indian boycott. The strength of American rivalry was shown by increasingly numerous purchases of British concerns in South America and in Britain itself.

The relative prosperity which some countries enjoyed after 1925 was pre-eminently industrial, but industrial activity in Britain during this period was never more than moderately good. In some of the main branches production did not even reach the pre-war level. "Up to 1929 we suffered from trade depression in many of our great industries, accompanied by a more or less steady figure of one million unemployed, at a time when other countries were enjoying a considerable share of prosperity."[1] In 1913 the estimated British consumption of raw cotton was over two million tons: in 1929 it was less than one and a half million tons. In the same period coal output fell from 287 million tons to 259 million tons. Foreign competition had kept the volume of export down to 80 per cent of their pre-war level. Between 1913 and 1929 our proportion of world coal output dropped

[1] *Report of the Committee on Finance and Industry* (The Macmillan Report. H.M. Stationery Office. Cmd. 3897, 1931. 5s.).

THE DECLINE OF BRITISH CAPITALISM 43

from 23·3 per cent to 18·8 per cent; of pig iron from 13·2 per cent to 7·8 per cent; of steel from 10·2 per cent to 8·1 per cent; of cotton consumption 18·6 per cent to 0·8 per cent.

With the coming of world crisis, the British official index of industrial production fell in the four years 1929–32 from 106 to 88. The figure for coal output in 1931 equalled that for 1900 and pig-iron production that for 1860. Exports fell from £729,000,000 to £389,000,000 between 1929 and 1931. The estimated net income from overseas investment fell from £250,000,000 in 1929 to £165,000,000 in 1930. Shipping earnings in the same period fell by more than 50 per cent. In September 1931 the British Government was forced off the Gold Standard.

Great Britain has undergone a heavy relative decline. As one competing unit among many, each of which is concerned to expand production, she has played her part in the precipitation of the general decline and crisis of world capitalism. The insistence upon profits, which is the basic principle of capitalism, has meant the disproportionate accumulation of capital and its embodiment in new means of production devized by advancing technique. The development of new technique reduces the number of workers employed and reduces the total wages paid for the operation of new machinery. The lower wage total and greater unemployment brings a narrowing market for consumption goods and presents the spectacle of a world in acute crisis because it cannot produce plenty without also producing poverty.

Britain, as the oldest of the competing groups, arrived at this stage of its development at an early date. By 1921 there were a million unemployed, and since that date mass unemployment has presented an insoluble problem. Even the so-called "boom" years of 1928 and 1929 showed more than a quarter of a million unemployed, while real depression brought the figure up to three millions. Mass unemployment has come to be officially accepted as a long-term characteristic of British capitalism. At the beginning of 1933 the Chancellor of the Exchequer announced that he calculated on the continuance of such unemployment for the next ten years. The Royal Commission on Unemployment estimated, for seven industries with one quarter of all insured workers, an excess of from 395,000 to 718,000 out of a total of 3,264,000. It anticipated the more or less permanent unemployment of three million workers. "It is now clear that the greater part of the unemployment of the period 1923 to 1929 was not due to trade depression, but was of a more persistent character due to causes that were not transient. . . . It is, of course, true that the present depression has involved workers who have every prospect of re-employment when industry generally improves. . . . But the difference remains that the unemployment caused by trade depression will pass, while the other unemployment will persist when trade improves, as it persisted through the good years 1924, 1927, and 1928 . . . associated with some more permanent condition of British industry."[1]

Before the war the existence of a small though increasing percentage of unemployed workers was looked upon as a normal characteristic of capitalism. It was

[1] *Royal Commission on Unemployment Insurance, Report* (1932), pp. 91–3.

THE DECLINE OF BRITISH CAPITALISM 45

implicit in financial expansion abroad and in the displacement of workers by technical advance. The pre-war industrial reserve army was part of the apparatus of expanding productivity; the absolute number of productive workers employed was increasing. But since the war the development of productive forces has produced mass unemployment and a direct reduction of the absolute number of workers employed. Post-war industrial development increased the total world productive capacity beyond the point at which the total equipment could find employment. While the actual volume of agricultural production has increased, "recent mechanical inventions have," in the words of the Macmillan Report, "created a problem of surplus labour in the agricultural regions of the world at a time when technical changes were tending to reduce the chance of employment in industry." Between 1913 and 1928 the increase in output per head of workers engaged in thirty principal industries in Great Britain was 33 per cent, but the increase in employment was 2·2 per cent—less than the increase in population, according to *The Times Trade Supplement*, July 23, 1932. In the post-war period alone the tendency is even more pronounced. Between 1923 and 1928 the number of insured workers in employment fell from 8,368,000 to 7,898,000, while the index of production on a 1913 basis of 100 rose from 88·7 to 96·3. Even before the advent of world crisis, therefore, employment fell 5·6 per cent against a 7·6 per cent rise in production.

Nor is that the whole story. To the contradiction between increasing production and decreasing employment must be added the contradiction between the growth of productivity and the decrease in the workers' share thereof. According to the *League of Nations' World Economic Survey* the percentage of the national income going to wages fell in the United Kingdom from 42·7 to 40·9. According to *The National Income 1924–31*, by Colin Clark, the output per employed person rose 13 per cent while the proportion of wages to home-produced income fell from 41·5 per cent to 38 per cent. Crisis has only accelerated this process. The need for rationalization, for the quickening-up of production, the ever greater output per man for an ever smaller return—these exigencies of competition have both grown severe under crisis and made crisis itself more acute.

What is to be done? Two millions of unemployed cannot be put back to work for there is no market for their product. Any increase of purchasing power resulting from a transference of some of the unemployed from the dole to wage-earning would be counterbalanced by a distribution of the increased volume of production which would, as always, be so favourable to profits, rent, interest, and royalties as to give a fresh impetus to investment and the development of productive capacity at a rate which would soon bring about further depression. The remedy for the capitalist dilemma does not lie in any direct attempt to reduce unemployment. As Mr. Baldwin said in the House of Commons on November 27, 1933: "There is a great core of unemployment. We do not know what the numbers may be. There may be a million, a million and a half, or less than a million; but there will be a vast number for whom there is but little hope of employment being found in this country. The gates of migration are closed against us. What can we do? That is a problem that has baffled the country completely up to now." The significance of this utterance lies in the first sentence, in the use of the word "core." Mr. Baldwin accepts the fact that the very heart of British capitalism is composed of a mass of hopeless unemployed.

Nothing, then, can be done about unemployment—beyond regretting the cessation of migration. Nothing can be done about narrowing markets, for that is the root of the whole trouble—the basic condition of capitalism in its latest stage. There remains one possibility: the curtailment of production, the bringing of the whole system to a standstill, the organization of decay. If productivity is too great for the market and if the sanctity of profits prevents any growth of the market, the only possible device is the restriction of productivity, the adjustment of wealth to poverty. That is the general "remedy" of capitalism; the remedy that is most efficiently applied in fascist states, where all opposition to it is carefully crushed by the violence of the mass fascist movement. Britain is not suffering from a crisis as acute as that which afflicts the German people. But in common with all other capitalist countries she has been visited by severe depression. And, over and above world depression and recovery, minor boom or no minor boom, she faces, and has for many years been facing, the inescapable fact of steady economic decline. It is, therefore, necessary to ask how far British capitalism has made up its mind to accept the end of expansion and to organize for decline; how far it has gone already along the road that leads to fascism.

IV

THE NEW ECONOMIC POLICY

IN 1930 the National Shipbuilders' Security, Ltd., was set up with power to borrow up to three million pounds, for the purpose—according to the Memorandum of Association —of assisting "the shipbuilding industry by the purchase of redundant and or obsolete shipyards, the dismantling and disposal of their contents, and the re-sale of their sites under restrictions against further use for shipbuilding." This company soon got to work, purchasing and closing down William Beardmore & Co.'s Dalmuir shipbuilding yard which during the war employed six thousand men. Up to the end of 1933 this new type of capitalist company had bought and closed down one hundred shipbuilding berths. In the twelve months to June 1933 the world tonnage of merchant shipping showed a net decrease of 1,814,000 tons, more than half this decrease being in tonnage owned by Britain. On August 4, 1934, the *New Statesman and Nation* reported: "Meanwhile in Britain as well the merry game of restricting the possibilities of future production goes on apace. Shipbuilders' Security, Ltd., has acquired from Armstrong Whitworth three more Tyne shipyards, which will presumably be so dismantled as to be put permanently out of action. With these three, eight out of fourteen Tyne shipyards will have disappeared, leaving only six in existence, and only four actually at work." But this is an imperfect world and we should weep with the *Economist* over the evil tidings of July 22, 1933: "Numerous attempts originating in this country, to reduce the world's shipping capacity and to raise freight rates by international scrapping and laying-up schemes, all ended in failure."

The Woolcombers' Mutual Association, Ltd., formed early in 1933, has as its object "to assist the woolcombing industry by the purchase and dismantling of redundant and obsolete mills, plant, and machinery for resale under restrictive covenants against their future use for woolcombing." After such organized destruction of basic industries comes the organized restriction of production of non-ferrous metals and foodstuffs. According to the *Statist* of March 11, 1933, the restriction scheme adopted by the Indian, Ceylon, and Dutch East Indies producers restricts initially the export of tea by 15 per cent of the maximum exported during the previous four years, with the result of a reduction of approximately £121,000,000 in exports. The *Statist* of May 13, 1933, reports an International Tin Committee as having, in 1932, finally united the Malayan and Bolivian producers in a scheme for severe restriction, directed at the "pruning" of the capacity of the tin industry to one-third by the middle of 1933. *The Times* of November 18, 1933, reports Sir Robert Horne as having said to the Imperial Smelting Corporation shareholders: "The International Zinc Cartel . . . established in 1931, has done very good service. At the inception of the Cartel a general remedy was applied to the general disease of over-production and increasing stocks; the result was very satisfactory. By the end of August 1933, stocks outside the U.S.A. had been reduced by 35 per cent."

In the business of restriction and destruction Britain has not been backward. All this, however, is but a beginning: much remains to be done. As Mr. G. S. Haskell, chairman of the Eastern Bank, Ltd., says: "If throughout the world the acreage of wheat, cotton, sugar, and rubber (British and Dutch) were decreased, if there were less drilling for oil, if subsidies for shipping were ruthlessly cut down, and steps to curtail production in other directions were taken, there would be every prospect of an advance in prices and a consequent trade revival" (*Statist*, April 1, 1933). Mr. Haskell should be of good cheer for he does not lack supporters. The Chancellor of the Exchequer, for example, was of opinion in the House of Commons on June 2, 1932, that: "To allow production to go on unchecked and unregulated in these modern conditions when it could almost at a moment's notice be increased to an almost indefinite extent was absolute folly" (*The Times*, June 3, 1933). The *Economist* of May 13, 1933, was no less ready to rejoice that "There can be little doubt that substantial progress has already been made in the readjustment of productive capacity to the lower level of demand for consumer's goods."

The idea of such "readjustment" may seem fantastic, from the angle of common sense. From the angle of capitalist survival, however, it is an absolute necessity and accepted as such. The only conceivable alternative to restriction and destruction in such industries as shipping and wool is the restoration of the markets, the restoration of world free trade. In fact, however, this is less an alternative than a pleasant dream. For as Mr.

John Strachey says: "It may be true that 'everybody' (that uninspiring abstraction) would be much richer in a free trade world. But that does not alter the fact that those very wealthy and influential capitalist gentlemen Herr Schmidt of Düsseldorf, Sir Algernon Smith of Birmingham, Henry T. Smith of Pittsburg, and M. Durand of St. Etienne, would all be immediately poorer. ... If the free trader economists, or anybody else, are to be given the power to scale down tariff barriers, they will be given the power, here, to bestow immeasurable wealth, there to deal destruction and ruin. They will be opposed by most powerful and well-organized forces, by the organized entrepreneurs of every state, fighting a life-and-death struggle for very existence."[1]

There was a time when a Britain that dominated the commercial and financial world could afford to worship at the shrine of Free Trade. But British Imperialism is a jealous god, and when in decline he is ill-disposed towards lesser deities. He sent his prophet among us in the troubled 'nineties, but with the coming of better times no one harkened unto the voice of Joseph. After many years, however, he comes into his own; the eyes of all men are opened to the inner truth of capitalism, which is the closed monopolist area. In the service of that truth the faithful must rally to the defence of their tribal god against the idolaters of other tribes. For has not Neville, the son of the prophet, said: "Much as all of us regret the economic warfare which has arisen between us and other countries, we must maintain that warfare as long as it is the other countries which have

[1] *The Coming Struggle for Power*, pp. 141-2.

taken the aggressive." And has not the high priest, Keynes, said: "let goods be homespun whenever it is reasonably and conveniently possible, and above all let finance be primarily national." And have not those heretics, the bankers, who even in 1926, in the face of all the signs and portents, called out of their ignorance for lower tariffs—have they not recanted and embraced the true faith, signing, in the second year of crisis, a manifesto saying that: "The immediate step for securing and extending the market for British goods lies in reciprocal trade agreements between the nations constituting the British Empire. As a condition of securing these agreements, Great Britain must retain her open market for all Empire produce while being prepared to impose duties on all imports from all other countries."

After destruction, the tariff. The second main policy of British capitalism in its fight for "recovery" is "protection," by which is meant the making of Britain into a monopoly market guarded by tariff walls, from behind which Mr. John Strachey's Sir Algernon Smith of Birmingham can laugh at Herr Schmidt of Düsseldorf, Henry T. Smith of Pittsburg, and M. Durand of St. Etienne.

An attempt was made at the Ottawa Conference to implement the policy of trade agreements within the Empire. Difficulties were, however, encountered and small concessions from the Dominions were gained only at the cost of much greater sacrifices from Britain. As regards India and the Crown Colonies, however, greater success has attended the effort to safeguard the interests of British firms. The Indian Government having agreed to give preference to British imports, the British manufacturer is now able to enjoy a more favourable position in the Indian market than his Japanese rival. And with the intensification of economic nationalism all over the world, British capitalism must, if it is to remain a Great Power, continue to extend tariffs round the whole Empire and to increase the area within which it can sell its products at protected prices. Such a policy will of course entail losses in Europe, but already many of Britain's former fields of economic activity, such as Germany, the U.S.A., and Russia, are largely closed to her.

In the absence of complete realization of this idea of imperial tariff unity, every effort must be made to make the best of the present situation. If we cannot be self-sufficient as an Empire, we must be self-sufficient as a nation. To the extent that we cannot do battle, as a closed imperial unit, for markets, areas of exploitation, and sources of raw material, we must proceed to the strengthening of our insular position. In order successfully to fight abroad we must close the home market. In Mr. Chamberlain's words: "We mean also to use it (the tariff weapon) for negotiations with foreign countries ... and we think it prudent to arm ourselves with an instrument which shall at least be as effective as those which may be used to discriminate against us in foreign markets." The National Government therefore provides itself with Import Duties, primarily for the purpose of bargaining for position and "disarming" the foreigner, while the special additional tariffs rising to 100 per cent are to be used for downright retaliation against rival users of tariffs. As Mr. Chamberlain says, they started it.

As a result there has been a redistribution of trade

within the Empire. Britain's purchases from the Empire in the first half of 1934 increased from 30·3 to 38·8 per cent of the total, while the exports to the Empire rose from 43·8 to 45·1 per cent of the total. After Ottawa the next task was the negotiation of trade treaties with foreign countries—chiefly Denmark, Norway, Sweden, Germany, and Brazil, with whom our tariff weapon enabled us to arrange mutual concessions. These agreements, however, brought an immediate and embarrassing response from within the Empire, to the distress of Lord Beaverbrook. Imports from Baltic and South American states having been limited, Canada, Australia, and New Zealand turned out to be so little observant of the decencies of Empire as to flood the English market with eggs, frozen meat, bacon, hams, wheat, barley, butter, and cheese. Such behaviour as this has carried the popular idea of self-sufficiency away from Empire and towards the nation. The farmers clamoured for tariffs against the Dominions and had their desires realized, in part, in the restriction of cattle imports from the Irish Free State and Canada. On the whole the Minister of Agriculture has been successful, with the help of tariffs, subsidies, agreements within the Empire, and the agricultural marketing Acts, in organizing new methods for regulating farm production, increasing prices, and raising the workman's cost of living.

Such measures as these have, it is claimed, brought a degree of recovery. It is certainly true that over the whole world industrial production has increased. But, as the Director of the International Labour Office, Mr. Harold Butler, says: "A new controversy is now breaking out among economists as to whether the improvement already effected has come about because of or in spite of the positive action taken by governments to promote it." Certainly it is exceedingly doubtful whether the claims of the National Government deserve recognition. The departure from the Gold Standard, which helped British trade, was not a deliberate but a forced departure which the government did all in its power to prevent. That the tariff did less damage to British foreign trade than had been expected was due to the partial offsetting of its effects by the simultaneous but involuntary devaluation of the pound. The signs of economic stability and even of improvement that Great Britain has shown are due largely to the operation of world factors, removed from the immediate control of the government, or to the skill and resources of the world's oldest and most experienced bourgeoisie.

But, however relatively privileged the position of Britain may be at the moment, there is no certainty that it will long remain so. Competition for export markets is already being renewed by Great Britain, Germany, and the United States, while the steady increase of Japanese exports will add more and more to British difficulties. In fact, in only one exporting industry is there a real hope of substantial prosperity. Great Britain holds first place among the four countries which have a virtual world monopoly of armament manufacture. The past few years have seen increased activity in steel, chemical, and aeroplane works. The Prime Minister, questioned in the House about activity in a time of general depression, maintained that it was all for "industrial purposes."

Which answers no questions. Why were the basic sources of "industrial purposes" showing substantial increases in output when there was no sign of a general revival in the manufacturing industries? Why do Imperial Chemical Industries receive millions in government money for the purpose of producing oil by coal-hydrogenation at a cost of two and one-third times the cost of producing natural oil? The new process will start no booms in the coal industry. It will, however, provide for oil supplies under conditions of war.

Direct state assistance to war industries is one factor in preparations for war that are taking on a new intensity. In the midst of the economic and political wilderness the National Government has taken the one certain line of policy compatible with the survival of Britain as an imperial Power. It is incorrect to say that the National Government has no foreign policy, as so many of the more ardent supporters of "collective security" are apt to do. On the contrary, the National Government has a very lively appreciation of the realities of a capitalist world. What else would Sir John Simon's policy be with regard to Japan but "tantamount to a formal repudiation of the Covenant," and the British Draft "a bad draft" and "ludicrously one-sided"?[1] The only wonder is that anyone should ever have supposed that the Covenant would not be repudiated when a world of economic imperialisms found itself in decline, or that any commonly acceptable Draft could be drawn up at a time when "peaceful" international conflict is more desperate than it has ever been.

[1] See *The Dying Peace*, by Vigilantes, pp. 6 and 14.

The National Government has, in fact, a twofold policy: the clearing away of the debris of liberal internationalism and the maintenance of the position of Great Britain as a Great Power. Most of the first half of this task has been accomplished, with the help of willing foreign hands. The real difficulty arises over the second half. Not only is foreign enthusiasm for it lacking, but there is also the problem of deciding which is the main chance, in order that the governmental eye may be kept on it. Clearly Japanese expansion, for example, if it goes too far, will beget anxiety, and much can be made of the argument that we can derive no real benefit from Japanese friendship, that Japan's motive in seeking a renewal of alliance is not to benefit the trade of others. On the other hand, the City, the Federation of British Industries, and the banks consider their investments in and trade with Japan sufficiently valuable to warrant the bringing of pressure to bear upon the National Government in the matter of sanctions against an aggressor. They are well aware of the motives behind Japanese aggression.[1] They know, in fact, that Japan is hungry, and, therefore, dangerously imperialist. Not being unfamiliar with the symptoms they do not make the mistake of supposing that a hungry Power will be bound by any Covenant. Knowing that Japan wants its hands free for war with the U.S.S.R. and later with the U.S.A. they seek realistically to arrange for the safety of their own possessions and for the supply of arms to Eastern theatres of war. The broad hint is given that expansion into Africa or Australia would have none of the advantages of expansion

[1] See supra, p. 26.

elsewhere. The Prime Minister can even offer at a Naval Conference to exchange the principle of parity (and American friendship) for British peace and quiet in the Far East. The British armament industry holds a key position in British counsels and in British economic structure, and if such an exchange can be made there is no reason why the National Government, the City, and sections of the Press should not turn an eye upon Japanese intentions towards the U.S.S.R. and the U.S.A. as blind as that which they turned upon the Japanese theft of Manchuria.

It is of course possible that the deal will not go through. To the extent, therefore, that the Japanese prove unreasonable in regard to British investments and possessions and legitimate aspirations, the National Government will have recourse to the one measure which is suitable for all eventualities—armaments. In the case of Japan the insurance would be in naval armaments. Hence the precautionary development of the Australian Navy and Air Force, the construction at Singapore, the Empire Defence Conferences, and an attitude on the part of the National Government towards the Naval Disarmament Conference of 1935 which takes full recognition of the needs of Imperial Defence. We want more ships and we want them smaller and cheaper.

Mr. Baldwin, in defending the Air Force increases in the House of Commons on July 29, 1934, said that a bigger Air Force is necessary to enable us to carry out our obligations and make our contribution to collective security. After paying this conventional lip-service he gave us a glimpse of the realities when he said that for the purposes of air defence our frontier is not the cliffs of Dover but the Rhine. In other words, the government, knowing exactly what German rearmament will mean, is insuring itself with a premium of five hundred new aeroplanes. It is, therefore, a mistake to say that the government has no foreign policy; on the contrary it is preparing with care and circumspection for several possible situations. Any grouping of capitalist countries is liable to dislocation for reasons inherent in the nature of a world society based on unequal capitalist development. The situation is complex, and it is not always easy for one country to determine its allies. But, in the meantime the National Government knows as well as any Mussolini that war is likely to be the continuation and the result of the policies with which each country seeks to meet crisis. At any moment some balance of power, some compromise effected between two or more competing nations as a lesser evil than facing the continued competition of another group—some such piece of diplomatic jugglery may break down. When that moment arrives it will be time to count the days before war breaks out.

If imperialist war is to be avoided and capitalism be made once again to prosper it will be necessary to bring about a restoration of the free market conditions upon which the successful working of capitalism depended in the past, and in the absence of which modern capitalism finds itself in crisis. Such restoration implies the removal of tariffs and all monopolistic and governmental interference with the spontaneous, automatic, and self-equilibrating movements of the "pure" capitalist system.

Unfortunately, however, no such purge is possible. In the international sphere freedom of trade had disappeared with the appearance of big trusts and monopolies, and no power can bring it back in the face of their opposition. The National Government, unlike its advisers of the "free marketeer" school, has accepted the obvious, and accepted it willingly. Realizing that to restore international free trade could only mean the bankruptcy of powerful sections of the community, it has very sensibly chosen to follow the inevitable course of capitalist development by pursuing a whole-hearted policy of tariffs and economic warfare.

In the domestic sphere, however, conditions are different. Here it is possible for a National Government to give satisfaction, in some degree, to those economists who desire the restoration of the free market. It might say to them: "We regret our inability to restore the conditions of a natural equilibrium by abolishing trusts and monopolies, which as you so rightly say help to cause crisis by the erection of tariff walls and the artificial maintenance of profits. It may be true that everybody would be much richer in a free trade world. But things being what they are, to attack monopoly would be to attack the strongholds of private property, and you should know, none better, that private property is the basis of our society, the thing we are here to preserve. Nevertheless, there is something we can do for you, and gladly. We entirely agree with you that the price of labour must, if capitalism is to flourish, respond with perfect freedom to supply and demand, and that trade unions and the apparatus of the social service state do much to check that free movement, preventing wages from falling to their natural level, reducing the rate of profit, and thus both helping to cause crisis and prevent recovery. And, since this is a time of crisis, we will take every possible measure to ensure that wages are reduced and as little additional income as possible is paid to labour in the form of social services. In conclusion may we express our thanks to you of the *laissez-faire* school for your very interesting justification of a policy which we had in any case decided to adopt."

Whether or not the orthodox school of economists play into the hands of a National Government makes no difference to British policy. Nor is it of importance, in the long run, whether they are right or wrong in their diagnosis—whether, that is to say, organized labour does help to cause crisis and retard recovery by preventing wage fluctuations and extracting social concessions. For whether trade unions exist or not, capitalism in distress must sacrifice everything rather than the flow of free income from private property.

The extent to which a capitalist country makes that attack, as a part of national policy, is a measure both of its distress and of its determination to achieve those purposes which are most completely achieved under fascism. While Britain is not yet fascist, there is no lack of evidence of the attempt to reduce every form of income paid to labour. The watchword since 1931 has been economy, meaning economy for small incomes. Wherever possible, the National Government cut wages and salaries, forced local authorities to do likewise, and invited private employers to follow its lead. It stopped or slowed down unemployment work schemes all over the country, and checked road and drainage projects, school and hospital building, and local development generally.

In addition, it saw fit to reduce unemployment benefit, to increase contributions, and to apply the notorious "Means Test," thereby handing over hundreds of thousands of genuinely unemployed men and women from unemployment insurance to the Poor Law, giving them the status of applicants for poor relief and submitting them to a written inquisition into the details of their domestic affairs and to a visitation from Poor Law officers seeking to discover every fact concerning means and standards of living. And, since the object of the Means Test is to transfer responsibility for the maintenance of the unemployed from the state to the family, an officer has not completed his duty until he has got into touch with the employer of any member of the family in work in order to check the earnings. If the claimant had no means and no one to maintain him he would receive under the conditions prevailing before the Unemployment Act of 1934 less than the full rate of benefit where the local poor relief scale was below the insurance benefit scale, as was the case in many areas.

As a result, and a not altogether surprising one, the full rates of "transitional benefit" were insufficient for adequate maintenance, especially in the case of long-term unemployment. But what is insufficient maintenance beside an annual saving to the "taxpayer" of fifteen million pounds? We must all make sacrifices, and, as the Prime Minister says, the National Government must

THE NEW ECONOMIC POLICY 63

explore every avenue. It must, in other words, be able to face its judges with the excuse of the man who, for sixpence, killed an aged woman: "Ah, Your Honour, sixpence here, and sixpence there, it all mounts up."

In July 1933 the Minister of Health told the House of Commons that there was no available medical evidence of any general increase in physical impairment, sickness, or mortality as a result of the economic depression or unemployment. This view was restated a few days later by the Parliamentary Secretary to the Board of Education, who said that not only was there no increase of malnutrition, but that "it appears on the whole that the tide has definitely turned." That remark was based on statistics which indicate that out of two hundred and sixty-eight reports for 1932 received from school medical officers only seventeen recorded increasing malnutrition. Only seventeen! Do not let us, therefore, judge the government too hastily; by 1932 many of the children cannot have been hungry for more than two years. Appearances are deceptive; as Dr. Kenneth Frazer, the Cumberland school medical officer, indicates, "a child may appear to be of normal height and weight and yet be in such a physical condition as to be susceptible to such epidemic diseases as influenza and probably to be in a condition in which the risk of laying the foundation of tubercular disease in later life may be a very serious issue."

Nor, it seems, were the two hundred and fifty-one officers who reported no increasing malnutrition being quite scientific in thus reassuring Mr. Ramsbotham. For the editorial of May 6, 1933, in the *Medical Officer*, the organ of the medical officers of health, argued that: "We must find out the clinical signs of malnutrition, for these we do not know. We know that at the present time a very large proportion of the population is imperfectly fed, but we cannot find the signs of it. We have districts where the amount spent on food is utterly inadequate to cover the necessities, and we report that observed nutrition of the children—who should be the most sensitive members of the community—is 90 to 95 per cent good. We know that this is false, and those who quote these results as proof that all is going well, that the British people in times of difficulty thrive excellently on bread and margarine—or coke—and are quite happy in doing so, know that it is false also."[1] Certainly it is false, but it is the only answer the National Government can make to its humanitarian critics. It cannot admit that capitalism has reached a stage of decline where it can maintain itself only by starving children. That would be too disturbing to the "taxpayer" and might "cause capital to leave the country." Nor can it admit that the children of the unemployed are of no consequence, because British capitalism will in the future be able to provide less work for them than it now provides for their fathers. That might provoke what used to be known in better times as "labour troubles." Nor can it make the one remaining answer—that since we fought a Great War with only one man in three up to the low standard of health required

---

[1] Quoted in *Labour Research*, September 1933. I have made considerable use of much of the valuable material on current economic and political developments that is to be found in these monthly circulars of the Labour Research Department.

THE NEW ECONOMIC POLICY 65

for foreign service, we need, therefore, have no qualms about economizing on cannon-fodder. That, in a government headed by an ex-pacifist and ex-socialist, might be a departure from good taste.

Early in 1934 there occurred a difference of opinion between the Ministry of Health and a Committee on Nutrition appointed by the British Medical Association on the question of the minimum food requirements of members of the working class. The dispute turned largely on where the truth lay between the Association Committee's report, which "found it impossible to prepare a diet for a child alone at a cost less than half a crown a week," and the Ministry's belief that the government's unemployment allowance of two shillings a week benefit for a dependent child is enough, not only for food, but for the other necessities of life as well. For those who care to investigate it there exists a mass of evidence,[1] mostly in the form of reports of medical officers of health, which indicates that the diet standards, both of the B.M.A. and the Ministry of Health, are inadequate, that our present-day knowledge of nutrition is insufficient for the planning of minimum diets compatible with health, and that even when minimum diets are planned for them, unemployed workers cannot afford them. Unemployment allowances were not sufficient in the first years of world depression. They are becoming even less so with the enforcement of a government policy which, by raising

[1] See a fully documented pamphlet entitled *Social Murder*, published by the Labour Research Department. See also chapter on "Nutrition" by Professor V. H. Mottram in *Time to Spare*, by Eleven Unemployed (Allen & Unwin).

E

food prices through quotas, restrictions, and subsidies, exploits the British consumer for the benefit of the British farmer. In the meantime, scientists dispute as to the minimum diet upon which a worker can maintain health and working capacity. There is never, be it noted, any suggestion of applying scientific knowledge to the provision of the best possible diet for improving his health and physique.

And if, in the name of economy and national self-sufficiency, even his physical welfare must be sacrificed, it is improbable that the education of his children will bulk large in the list of social responsibilities. A Great Power that cannot afford to feed its children certainly cannot afford to educate them. If, as in 1931, when expenditure on education was at its highest, it amounted in Britain to only 2·6 per cent of the estimated national income, it is unlikely that education will be especially favoured when, as in 1932, depression gives rise to a call for economy. Hence the reduction in November 1932 of expenditure on education by £6,000,000 a year, and the subsequent further economies under Circular 1421 such as the abolition of free secondary schools, the raising of secondary school fees, and the substitution of special places for free places. Hence the throwing of four-fifths of the rising generation onto the labour market when they have reached the age at which the children of another class are just beginning their serious education. Private enterprise, private property, and private profit demand the freedom of the labour market, which, for children, means casual labour, systematic exploitation by firms which dismiss successive relays of children as each batch demands higher wages. It means, first, blind-alley employment and then the long search for work in the face of the diminishing capacity of industry to absorb them. What better way of restoring freedom to the labour market than to maintain mass unemployment among children? For, as Professor Tawney has shown,[1] it is not only juvenile workers who are thus "freed." "An increase in the number of young persons competing for work tempts employers to make an increased use of juvenile labour. It is possible that part of the rise in juvenile unemployment, which is otherwise to be expected, may be averted by the substitution in industry of juvenile for older workers. That alternative is hardly, if at all, less disastrous. It means that the swollen torrent of boys and girls scrambling for jobs will be felt, not only by them, but by their elders. Unemployment among the latter is like to be aggravated and the downward pressure on the wage-standard of adults will be intensified."

By providing for the establishment of juvenile instruction centres the government has committed what Professor Tawney calls "the fundamental absurdity of providing education—of a sort—only for those children who are unemployed at the moment of their unemployment." It has preferred to do this rather than to raise the school-leaving age to fifteen, which, as the Association of Education Committees has said many times, would better serve the educational and economic interests of the community. Two reasons were given for refusal to raise the school-leaving age. It would cost £8,000,000 in maintenance allowances and it would not seriously diminish juvenile

[1] *The School-leaving Age and Juvenile Unemployment*, p. 8.

unemployment. It is interesting to compare the first reason with the cost of armaments, over £100,000,000, and the second with the Ministry of Labour figures which estimate that raising the leaving age would take 355,000 children off the labour market. But the moral of such comparisons, while significant enough to the humanitarian, has no reference to the purpose of the National Government. Britain's survival as a Great Power does not depend on the educational standards of working-class children. It does depend, however, on British capacity to compete with other Great Powers in armaments, and in a world market where low costs of production, such as may be achieved by an excess of labour supply over demand, are the secret of success.

With such conditions in mind, the National Government could clearly make no concessions in the matter of education. Indeed, it found itself forced to withdraw concessions. In May 1934 it was asked why it had refused permission to a number of local education authorities who wished to use their statutory power to raise the school-leaving age by local action. Here again two reasons were given: that the Board of Education was not satisfied that the requisite facilities were available in some of the areas, and that the areas were not isolated enough to make it desirable for the age to be raised in one area without being raised in the other. This surely was not up to the government's usual standard. It amounts to saying that we can do nothing to help education because education needs help. It is both disingenuous and lacking in the simple force of the reason noted above, which is simply that the first allegiance of the government is to private property.

The Board practised to deceive, however, only in the matter of the reasons for its action. No attempt was made to disguise the methods by which it took action. In making it impossible to raise the leaving age in any one area until such time as it is raised in all areas it took away, by an executive stroke of the pen, the power of local education authorities by Act of Parliament. The National Government in fact has rapidly acquired the habit of regimentation. Once it has made up its mind to economise on some social service, it sees no reason to stop for the nice observance of democratic forms. If local authorities become troublesome—silence them by administrative order. If the able-bodied unemployed present a problem, herd them into what one of His Majesty's Ministers, among others, called concentration camps. This was probably what the Prime Minister meant when he said to the National Labour Committee on November 6, 1933: "The secret of the success of dictatorships is that they have managed somehow or other to make the soul of a nation alive. . . . In this country the three parties in co-operation are doing that, and our task must be to get the young men with imagination, hope, and vision behind us." What better way for the National Government to get the imagination, the hope, the vision of the unemployed behind them—well behind them—than to borrow that most successful institution of dictatorship, the concentration camp. A start was made under the Poor Law Acts with the "training centres," both day and resident, at which physical training and educational and vocational tuition were provided for men on relief. Then under the Unemployment Act of 1934 this system was extended, with all the original evils retained, and some new ones added, notably an element of compulsion in that the granting of relief may be made conditional on attendance at a training camp.

There is no reason to believe that the camps will become any less objectionable or more educational than they have hitherto been proved to be. There is, however, no reason to believe that in the interests of the buyers of cheap labour the government is attempting to offset a few years' undernourishment and demoralization by a few weeks of disciplined life in the open air. The watchword is economy, which means that property must economize at the expense of labour. The Budget of 1934 reduced Income Tax by £24,000,000, the Motor Duty by £4,000,000, restored £5,500,000 in salary cuts, and £8,000,000 in unemployment allowances. That was one side of the picture as painted by that master of knife work Mr. Chamberlain. The other side was a two months' delay in the restoration of the unemployment cuts and an indication of the provisions of the Unemployment Bill, which, when passed, preserved the household Means Test, transferred the function of assessment from local bodies to an irresponsible Unemployment Assistance Board, threw back on the worker the duty of proving that he is genuinely seeking for work, and threatened anything from disallowance of benefit to compulsory attendance at training camps.

The essence of the government's policy is to remedy

capitalist distress at the expense of the one part of the economic system that can be sacrificed without serious danger to the whole. In the three years since the Doctor's Mandate was asked for and given, the treatment has been exceedingly drastic. Leaches have been applied and amputations performed. Naturally the knife has been used, for the most part, only where the flesh was thin. If it was only the undernourished parts of the system that were called upon to give blood, that was merely in order that the richer and therefore more vital parts might gain by the transfusion. And it was clearly essential that Sir Thomas Inskip be called in to safeguard the areas thus weakened from contact with anything calculated to poison or inflame. Whether such treatment is likely to promote recovery is quite beside the point; under capitalist conditions it is both right and inevitable, there is no other treatment which would not check the lifegiving flow of free income.

The necessity for economy is recognized by the business man no less than by the politician. Inspired by the example of a government which is able to relieve the rich man's burden by reducing state wages and every form of social income, the business man applies himself afresh to wage-cuts and the speeding up of the productive process. Further to strengthen his position he proceeds next to attack the co-operative movement. He is not satisfied with the National Government's Finance Act of 1933, which claims income tax on the reserve allocations of co-operative societies. Through the good offices of Lords Beaverbrook and Rothermere, the National Citizens' Guild and the Municipal Reformers, he demands taxation of co-operative dividends, the abolition of dividend on the sale of milk, and a prohibition on the establishment of any new branch co-operative store except after inquiry by a government official. He is in fact organizing a little fascism on his own. Eager to destroy working-class organizations that threaten his trusts, he uses the newspaper, in which the trusts, unlike the co-operatives, advertise extensively, to instil into small shopkeepers the fear of a rising proletariat which will crush them, the while he is himself absorbing them by purchase or the force of bankruptcy. Such a tactic is of the essense of fascism—a movement, middle class in personnel, fears, and ostensible purpose, but capitalist in direction and real purpose. It bears most of the significant characteristics of its continental models. If it were an isolated adventure of a group of exceptionally property-conscious Press Barons and business men, it might be disregarded as a mere straw showing which way the wind would like to blow. But it is not an isolated adventure. Inasmuch as it is an attempt to achieve fascist objectives it is merely one example among many. The restriction and destruction of productive capacity, the tariff policy, and the movement towards national self-sufficiency and rearmament, the Unemployment Act, the economy made in wages and in every field of social service—all these are no less fascist in purpose than the attack on co-operative associations. In its economic aspect fascism is essentially an attempt on the part of private property to improve its position at the expense of labour. That the new economic policy of British capitalism is less ruthless towards labour than the policy of Hitler or

Mussolini is merely because the position of property in Britain leaves less to be desired than did the position of property in the immediately pre-fascist Germany or Italy. The difference in the degree of ruthlessness does not, however, obscure the identity of purpose. And when British capitalism finds itself in distress comparable to that of Germany and Italy it will also find it necessary to bring about the complete or fascist subjugation of labour.

V

THE WITHDRAWAL OF BRITISH DEMOCRACY

THE problems which face a distressed capitalism are not exclusively economic. The attempt to sacrifice labour to property will, in a democratic society, encounter the political opposition of those who deny the virtue of the remedies chosen by capitalism and of those who assert that a system which adopts such remedies had better be superseded. Such opposition cannot, however, be permitted by a capitalism which is convinced of the necessity of reaction in the economic sphere. In the name of private property it dare not allow that slackening of the flow of free income which would result from successful political challenge to its economic policies. A capitalism in distress must, therefore, obtain freedom of action; it must make an attack upon its political opponents and upon the organizations and institutions through which their opposition is carried on. Where crisis is acute the demand for a free hand is urgent and, if opposition to reaction is strong, the result is fascism with its complete destruction of every political principle and association by which labour seeks to defend itself. Where crisis is less acute and where opposition to capitalist policy is less powerful, a less drastic assault upon democratic institutions and working-class organizations will suffice to give property the free hand it desires. In any case, if the economic expansion which permitted the establishment of democratic institutions, with their inevitable drive towards equality, comes to an end, and is replaced by a process of contraction, we may expect, in one degree or another, that those institutions will be withdrawn.

No one supposes that democratic institutions are the private property of the working class. Modern political democracy is historically the product of many interrelated forces, of which the most powerful were those changes of forms of production known as the Industrial Revolution. A new and growing manufacturing and commercial middle class found its ambitions denied and its activities limited by the political and economic domination of a privileged landowning aristocracy. The answer to privilege was found in liberal philosophy and democratic institutions. The school of Bentham provided both, demonstrating the virtue of rational individualism and the expediency of representative democracy as the instrument of virtue. The new combination overcame political privilege just as the new productive forces proved too much for the farming interest. The new politics and the new economics found favour in each other's sight. No one could forbid the banns and so they went hand in hand through the nineteenth century, with only an occasional voice to suggest a latent incompatibility which would one day bring their grey hairs in sorrow to the divorce court. With economic expansion came material progress, and with material progress grew the popularity of the political system which apparently maximized the role of the individual in government enterprise while minimizing the role of government in individual enterprise.

During the prosperous period of British capitalism there was room for both Conservative and Liberal in a

Parliament which was content to keep the ring for an individualism synonymous with rising standards of living. Both parties were in substantial agreement about the fundamental rightness of British society, both believed in free competition, private enterprise, and private profit. Differences between them were differences of more or less, faster or slower, never of kind or of general direction. "Both parties were in substantial agreement upon the vital importance of liberal individualism, especially in the industrial realm; both refused to see the state as more than a supplementary corrective of the more startling deficiencies of individual execution. They could afford their differences of opinion because, as in the relationships of a family, these were based upon those substantial identities of outlook which make compromise possible at all pivotal points."[1]

It was all very well for the high priests of *laissez-faire* to confine themselves to the correction of startling deficiencies while standards of living were rising. But when British economic expansion began to encounter obstacles in the last quarter of the nineteenth century the working class began to suggest that the state should assume the responsibilities which the economic system could no longer discharge. It was only natural that men reared in the tradition of rising standards should expect to receive in social services those increasing benefits which a crumbling supremacy could no longer afford in wages. From the standpoint of economic theory it was, of course, an abysmally unscientific expectation, even allowing for the fact that the work of von Mises of Vienna, which

[1] H. J. Laski, *Democracy in Crisis*, pp. 34–5.

shows it to be impossible, was then not yet available. The slightest acquaintance with the works of the classical school should have been sufficient to demonstrate the unwisdom of taxing industry to pay for social services at a time when it was becoming increasingly necessary, in the face of foreign rivalry, for British capitalism to economize on the payments made to labour. Unfortunately, however, the state was not at liberty to take the advice of the classical school. As has so often happened with the disciples of Ricardo, their advice, though sound, was irrelevant. For industry to be held up to ransom for the benefit of the working class might be in the long run the worst thing that could happen to both, but British capitalism was concerned with a more immediate problem. It had established democratic institutions as a means of abrogating privilege, and it was beginning to discover that aristocratic privilege was not the only kind that those institutions could abrogate. In its struggle with the landowning class it had enlisted the common man, armed him with the vote, and paid him in material progress. Now it was beginning to wonder whether the common man, denied any further material progress, might take advantage of his democratic institutions to discuss the question of economic privilege. And that was not the kind of discussion in which the owners of economic power cared to engage. Nevertheless, it was becoming increasingly obvious that in political democracy there is implicit a drive towards economic equality. It had been found necessary to offer "a share in political authority to all citizens upon the unstated assumption that the equality involved did not seek extension to the economic sphere. The assumption could not be maintained."[1] There was only one solution—to keep the question of ownership and control of economic power off the agenda by satisfying the shareholders with a bonus in the form of socialistic reform. And having taken the decision it only remained for the directors to bid the classical economists a sorrowful farewell and put them on the train for Vienna.[2]

So, for a time, the loyalty of the working class was obtained in return for a new social service state, paid for out of the surplus wealth of what had been, and would no longer be, a world industrial monopoly. Property, by submitting itself to various kinds of increasingly severe taxation, provided a background in which English socialism became Fabian rather than Marxian in theory, gradualist rather than revolutionary in practice.

It was a clever solution, but it had two related disadvantages. It was a decade or so late, and it was too expensive. It should have been adopted in the 'sixties when British capitalism would have been better able to afford it. British capitalism would have been better advised to pay for a substantial instalment of social services out of the revenue of the unchallenged monopoly of the 'sixties. As it was the concessions were made with a bad grace at a time when British capitalism had ceased to expand, and when their cost had to be met

[1] Laski, *Democracy in Crisis*, p. 53.
[2] Someone, however, must have bought them a return ticket, for they are back in the shape of Professor Hayek, at one time of Vienna, now at the University of London, saying, now that both wages *and* social services are being reduced: "We told you so."

out of the proceeds of a diminishing share of world trade. And, once begun, both processes made great strides. One concession led to another, the more property paid in ransom the more it was asked to pay; one foreign competitor was added to another, and the more manufactures industry offered in exchange for foodstuffs and raw material the more it was asked to offer.

In such circumstances it cannot be long before property becomes convinced of the urgent necessity of calling a halt to the policy of concessions. But although it can state that necessity as a simple matter of national solvency, it cannot thereby convince a working class brought up to expect an increasing flow of social income. The business of conviction is difficult because the working class knows that an increasing social expenditure is the one thing that makes tolerable its worsening position in the labour market. Its natural reaction to a stabilized or decreasing social expenditure is resentment directed towards its economic status and towards the assumptions upon which that status is based. When concessions cease, the demand for concessions does not grow less; rather it is reinforced by a demand for equality not as and when capitalism can afford it but as of right. In reversing the trends of its social policy, property finds itself opposed not only by the reformism of the trade unions but also, if only in a small way, by the socialism of those who are convinced of an inescapable contradiction between social needs and the working of capitalist distribution.

It is, however, easy to read into this picture more than is in fact there. The convinced socialists are a very small minority without effective access to the rank and file of the working class. The reformists subscribe formally to a socialist programme, though with many reservations as to time and opportunity. The demand for concessions does not grow weaker, but there is no determination to carry the demand to the point of presenting a final challenge to capitalist assumptions. Labour policy is in essence the conviction that socialism can be achieved gradually, and that in default of its immediate realization more concessions will be obtained by co-operating with capitalism than by holding a pistol to its head. In so far as this policy meant acquiescence in the plans of capitalism there was no problem for property to solve in the post-war period. If labour wished to co-operate in rationalization, in rebuilding and reorganizing capitalism, no less a person than Sir Alfred Mond would be willing to discuss ways and means. More than willing, in fact, for if working-class loyalty to capitalism could be bought at the cost of a little profit sharing, a little co-partnership, a few Mond-Turner conferences, it would be cheap at the price. In so far as labour advocated the public corporation as a form of socialism, the Conservative party saw nothing to object to. The London Passenger Transport Act represented nothing more than formal recognition of the trend of industry towards monopolistic forms. A Conservative Government was perfectly willing to enact much of the substance of Mr. Morrison's Bill. As *The Times* said, "Where does the socialism come in?" Had not a Conservative Government already set up a Central Electricity Board and an Imperial Communications Company? But in so far as labour was so precipitate as to use the fact of rationalization as a basis for the demand of substantial concessions, then, so far from there being any possibility of co-operation, there could be only conflict pierced by the wails of those distressed by the inability of labour to face the facts of international competition.

The wailing grew louder when labour in office proceeded to ruin the country in a very real sense. Property discovered that labour understood so little of what was implied in the "reorganization of capital" that it could choose a decade of industrial depression, with its long series of strikes at home and steady losses in foreign markets, as a suitable period in which to put through large and expensive schemes of social reform. The second Labour Government was indeed forced in the end to realize that there are, or should be, limits to taxation in a time of severe depression. Becoming fearful for the national finances they appointed a committee under Sir George May to examine them. The examination revealed that without drastic measures of economy there would be a deficit of £120,000,000 for the year 1932–3. The Cabinet realized after investigation that economy meant, among other things, raising unemployment contributions, restricting insurance benefits to twenty-six weeks in the year, reducing the pay of the police, members of the armed forces, and teachers, and reducing the expenditure on roads and grants under the Unemployment Grants Scheme.

The record of the National Government has shown that it has a very lively realization of the causes of the budgetary crisis of 1931. Looking back over the previous ten years it sees the error of a policy of concessions in a period of depression. It knows that a harassed profit system, so far from making new concessions, must withdraw old ones. Since British industrial supremacy was first challenged sixty years have passed; sixty years during which British capitalism has been slowly reaching the point where it can make no further advance towards the social service state—where, indeed, it must reverse the policy of co-operation which had been so successful in its reduction of British socialists to an eager band of co-operators, and so nearly disastrous in its assumption that they knew what co-operation meant.

Once the decision to reverse the policy of concessions has been made there ceases to be any ground for compromise between property on the one hand and reformism on the other. It had never, even in the best years, been possible to find common ground for debate between the Conservative (or Liberal) and the Socialist. To-day it is not even possible to find common ground between the Conservative and the seeker after reforms. What was possible in prosperity cannot be contemplated in depression.

Sections of the Labour party are still prepared to "co-operate," but if they have not learnt their lesson the same cannot be said of the owners of economic power. They know that to grant further concessions is to invite their own extinction. The Liberal no less than the Conservative knows that the challenge of a gradualist Labour party is, "socialism in our time" on one side, an attack upon the fundamentals of private ownership and private profit which are the root of capitalist society.

It is not necessary to find socialism in the Labour party programme in order to realize that there is a conflict between its purposes and those of private property which cannot be settled constitutionally. The nineteenth-century success of the British Parliamentary system was based upon the acceptance by each party of the other's legislation. Neither wanted to change the basic institutions of capitalist society. But when opposition comes from a Labour party, which in so far as it is socialist seeks to transform capitalism and in so far as it is reformist cannot in depression do other than ruin it, it is unlikely that property will see anything sacred in constitutional procedure, or anything to be gained by submitting vital differences to the verdict of the parliamentary system.

If the governing class cannot tolerate the demands of either socialism or reformism, neither can it look with any favour upon the machinery of representative democracy through which those demands are presented. Its attitude towards democratic institutions is at best doubtful and at worst uncompromisingly hostile. Nor does it find criticism of the parliamentary system a difficult task. There is no lack of evidence to show that the democratic method is largely impotent to deal with the vital questions of policy. Nor is there lacking a widespread conviction that the conditions in which the democratic method can be expected adequately to function are not present in post-war Britain. When, therefore, a member of the National Government seeks to bring parliamentary government into disrepute by denouncing the party system he does not have to look far for material nor for an audience already more than half-convinced that he is right.

He can point out that Parliament has become a mere institution for presenting that distasteful exhibition, the class struggle. He can argue that whereas its classical function was the making of decisions through discussion and debate, in modern times there is nothing to discuss. For if property submits to the parliamentary method, and refuses, as it must refuse, to grant concessions, the result sooner or later will be a Labour victory at the polls. As the protests grow louder against economy cuts, against the Means Test, and every other attempt to lower the standard of living, so propaganda increases for a National Government above mere party interests. While representative democracy remains, property faces a dilemma—it must either ruin itself by granting concessions which it cannot afford, or allow itself to be ruined a little more thoroughly by a Labour Government. True, the last Labour Government was called to order in time to avert disaster, but property has too much at stake to be able to gamble on future May Reports.

If the traditional democratic forms have ceased to operate as an effective safety-valve against the accumulation of social discontent, if property dare not submit vital issues to parliamentary decision, what reason remains for retaining the machinery of Parliament? If the important decisions must be taken without reference to majority opinion there can be no sense in going through formalities of debate which are meaningless and which cost money and time. The advocates of a single "national" party can point out, moreover, that the wheels of parliamentary debate, at best, grind both too slow and too small. Too slow because the economic problems which constitute the bulk of modern legislative work require rapid decision, based upon expert knowledge to which the average M.P. cannot pretend. And too small because large decisions have become the province of the Cabinet. Such large decisions, that is to say, as are ever submitted to democratic procedure have become the province of the Cabinet.[1]

When the "national" spokesman denounces Parliament as a dangerous concession-extracting device and an inefficient method of economic administration he will find many on the Conservative side to agree with him. Nor will he lack for Labour support on the second charge. And, with the difference that they would prefer to write "unsatisfactory" for "dangerous," an increasing number of Labour supporters will echo his first charge. For there is growing disillusionment with a party which can remain largely reformist after the disaster of 1931, and which will, therefore, as soon as it precipitates another budgetary crisis, be forced either to adopt a reactionary policy or to resign. A million or more votes of those disgusted with a Labour parliamentarism which could neither grant concessions nor administer capitalism efficiently went to swell the "National" poll. True, Labour has regained much of its former strength, but there are many who will not give it another chance, and, of those who do, once more will probably be enough.

The National Government may not have gone the

[1] For some recent illustrations of the fact that democracy in Britain always recognizes its proper limitations, see H. N. Brailsford, *Property or Peace?* pp. 76, 77.

whole way towards abandoning the parliamentary for the one-party method, but then the crisis of 1931 could have been worse than it was. In this connection it is worth while to examine the history of British coalitions in crisis in order to discover, for future reference, the manner in which disillusionment and panic can be harnessed and put to work by those faced with the possibility of having to exchange old safety-valves for new.

When in 1914 a hard spell of imperialism brought war, it brought also a Coalition Government. At that time the Labour movement was less socialist in character than it is now. It saw no reason to suppose that capitalist reformism was not a perfectly good policy for the working class to adopt. The Liberals had used it for many years with great success, and if they could no longer afford it, well, the Labour party was not too proud to buy second-hand goods. Nor did it expect immediate delivery. There was a war, and in those days Labour leaders, unlike the 1931 Cabinet, were not the men to forget that though it is permitted to suck the capitalist orange it is better to desist before the pips squeak. Being so observant of the decencies of extraction, they were welcomed into the first Coalition Government.

Nor was the party system the only section of the British political structure to be remodelled to suit the purposes of crisis. As soon as Parliament ceased to provide an effective opposition it ceased to command the attention or respect of the Cabinet. Mr. Lloyd George found it a waste of time to lead a House which had little to occupy itself with beyond the recording of assent to his policies. The meaning of the "flexibility" of the constitution was amply demonstrated by the passage of the Defence of the Realm Act, which bent, twisted, and stretched it into such a shape that it could conveniently be wielded by the executive alone.

For a short period after the war the working class so far forgot itself as to become almost revolutionary. Taking the offensive it gave property one of the worst scares it has had in modern times, presented it with a crisis of war-time severity, and forced it to take refuge in a second Coalition Government. Between the end of the Second Coalition and 1931 property was undecided which course it should take. Should it adopt the wartime expedient of welcoming the Labour movement into the fold or should it continue the policy of the Second Coalition and prepare for direct conflict? In the effort to discover which method, co-operation or subjection, would best deprive the movement of its capacity to do harm, property tried first one and then the other. Disguised coalitions in the form of Labour minority rule were twice given a trial. At other times uncompromising hostility seemed the best plan. Decidedly it seemed the best plan after the second Labour Government had succeeded in ignoring for two years the plain economies of a capitalism in distress. Expenditure on social services, together with the effects of depression upon national revenue, had proceeded to a point where an exceedingly difficult problem in budget-balancing had to be solved. British capitalism, choosing the bankers as its mouthpiece, informed the Labour Cabinet that it would not be possible to balance the budget without reducing unemployment insurance benefits. The situation seemed to compare in gravity with that at the outbreak of war. Labour was offered the choice of economizing and thereby following its gradualism to a logical conclusion or of proceeding into the political wilderness. A majority of the Cabinet chose temporarily to forsake logic, but their reasons for this course as given to the electorate did less to convince them than to add to an already strong atmosphere of panic. That atmosphere was carefully stimulated throughout the General Election. On all sides the spokesmen of capitalism pointed out that to refuse to reduce unemployment benefits was to go off the Gold Standard. The electors of Great Britain were submitted to a deluge of propaganda urging that to elect a Labour Government was to invite financial chaos. The pound, the interest on the National Debt, Post Office savings, and the City were declared to be in danger. The Right knew it to be impossible to create panic by showing that a Labour Government would not balance the Budget. It was necessary to go further and demonstrate that if Labour were elected every kind of financial disaster would follow.

The threat to ruin any popularly elected government which did not balance the Budget was not the only instance in 1931 of a constitutional convention put under a severe strain. It might have been expected that the King would follow the conventional path after Mr. MacDonald had made it clear that he could no longer hold his government together. The normal exercise of the royal functions would have entailed asking Mr. Baldwin, as leader of the Opposition, to form a government. The King preferred to ask Mr. MacDonald to form a National Government.

THE WITHDRAWAL OF BRITISH DEMOCRACY 89

Nor was the part played by the Prime Minister during the crisis without its constitutional peculiarities. It is customary for the British Prime Minister to confer with the members of his Cabinet on the question of a decision to give up the seals of office, or to ask the King for a dissolution. Mr. MacDonald, however, chose to take his decisions personally, without informing some members of his Cabinet. It would seem that Mr. MacDonald had no difficulty in discovering a new parliamentary practice which was both extremely interesting to the student of constitutions and useful to Mr. MacDonald. Crisis led him to move away from that form of Cabinet wherein the Prime Minister is first among equals towards a more presidential form in which the Prime Minister is first among subordinates.

Perhaps it is a little naïve to wonder at Mr. MacDonald's departure from convention in the matter of taking the Cabinet into his confidence. For, after all, it is of no great importance whether a man observes certain niceties of conduct if he is at the same time engaged in leaving a sinking ship. It is much more important to ask upon what rules Mr. MacDonald based his refusal, when he could command only a fractional support, to accept the decision of his party and to give the seals of office into other hands. Upon what code of morals did he base that denial of the traditions of the British party system which allowed him to abandon his party without notice and to become the head of a Coalition opposition more than ready to present itself as a suitable candidate for power?

In such circumstances the defeat of labour was a simple matter. Labour's record was its own worst enemy, for when the electorate heard the word "socialism" uttered from a Labour platform they felt that if its meaning was the meaning given to it in the last two years it was a bad thing, and that if it meant something else it was a pity that they had not been made aware of the fact before.

The party managed, however, to obtain 30 per cent of the votes cast which, curiously enough, gave it 8·4 per cent of the seats. Parliament was able, therefore, to assemble in the true war-time atmosphere. Britain was in danger, but she would be governed on "non-party" lines by a coalition formed without the slightest regard to the traditional conventions of party government. The constitutional example set by the nimble Prime Minister proved infectious. The next convention to be flouted was that of collective Cabinet responsibility. It has long been the custom for Cabinet Ministers to resign upon the rare occasions when they found themselves unable to speak or vote with the majority of their colleagues. But flexible as ever, the constitution was bent to accommodate the three free-trade members of the National Cabinet who, proud of their totalitarian outlook on all other matters, could not bring themselves to vote with their fellow Ministers on such a trivial and un-national issue as the government's Tariff Bill. The implications of such collective jugglery have been well noted by Mr. Lindsay Rogers. He asks why the principle of collective responsibility cannot be scrapped in respect of any other issue on which there is a difference of opinion. "Why could not the British Cabinet retain office with dissentient members in respect of disarmament policy, reparations, or the British debt to the United States? If the principle on which the MacDonald government acted were accepted in full, the leaders of the Labour opposition in the House of Commons could be taken into the Cabinet because they approved some non-controversial Bills which were part of the National Government's programme. Differences of opinion within the state could then be confined to differences of opinion within a single party, as is the case with the Fascist party."[1]

From the Crown to the Press, all sections of society had joined to meet crisis with the old totalitarian remedy. In short, British capitalism had obtained a free hand. The government gave itself new powers to delegate legislation to nominated bodies, and to increase the amount of legislation delegated to Ministers. It had in fact won the power to reorganize the economic condition of Britain without submitting its projects to any significant parliamentary examination. As the executive of a harassed capitalism it could without interference take up new weapons for an economic war in which Britain had for some time been losing ground. Its position has been neatly summed up by Mr. Brailsford. "The forms of democracy were preserved, but something also of the authoritative procedure of fascism was attained, and without the trouble of dressing in coloured shirts. What had been done for the defence of the realm was repeated for the defence of capitalism, and no one was startled or shocked. The English alone possess the art of making the boldest constitutional changes without raising their voices by the fraction of a tone."[2]

[1] Lindsay Rogers, *Crisis Government*, p. 81.
[2] Brailsford, *Property or Peace?* p. 60.

It is the good fortune of British capitalism that it has so far only needed to adopt a part of the authoritative fascist procedure. It has been able to achieve its purposes—the partial subjugation of the working classes —without resort to anything glaringly undemocratic. That does not, however, disguise the fact that its purpose is essentially fascist. The basic conditions for fascism exist when economic decline, which has united the old capitalist parties, develops into crisis and presents an imperative demand for capitalist rule if capitalism is to survive. For, however much a liberal reformism may be allowed access to power in better times, there can be no possibility in crisis of any compromise, political or economic, between the interests of the Labour party, the co-operative societies, and the trade unions on the one hand, and the interests of the owners of property and economic power on the other.

Previous governments have met working-class demands that seemed severely to threaten property interests with an Emergency Powers Act, an Organization for the Maintenance of Supplies, a Trades Union Act, or military demonstrations. These, in crisis, are not enough. External dangers and difficulties are worse than they have been since the war, and property knows that another spell of labour rule on reformist lines would, in the face of those external conditions, spell disaster. There will, therefore, be no more attempts to co-operate with labour. There is no alternative compatible with capitalist survival to keeping the working class in subjection. Which means that there is no alternative to what in Germany, Italy, and Austria is regarded as the fundamental rule of government.

THE WITHDRAWAL OF BRITISH DEMOCRACY 93

There is nothing in the record of the National Government to suggest that it is unaware of the importance of that rule or that it has experienced any difficulty in discovering measures for its application. Much, it was thought, could be done by reorganizing the police under more centralized forms. The Police Bill was introduced, which included among its provisions the limitation of the membership of the Police Federation to ordinary inspectors and lower ranks, the restriction of the period of service for constables to not more than ten years, and the training of upper ranks in a police college. In addition to providing in this way for a large nucleus of class-conscious and loyal police the National Government has with some success attempted to inspire the whole force with a new conception of duty. At the fascist meeting at Olympia police refused to interfere in cases of assault, either because they did not witness the actual assault or because they occurred on private property, notwithstanding that the law gives the police full powers to enter any such meeting and prevent such violence as occurred. While permitting fascist violence of an extreme nature against members of the audience they were active in interfering to prevent any demonstration outside Olympia against the Blackshirts and in taking into custody those who resented their attitude. The majority of prosecutions following upon the Olympia meeting were against persons not in sympathy with the Blackshirt movement, and there was a strong tendency on the part of magistrates to take the point of view—contrary to law—that a person who witnesses a dangerous assault is not at liberty to do his best to prevent it. This attitude may be contrasted with that of the police in working-class areas such as Glamorgan, which is much more generous in its interpretation of the law regarding the right of police entry. The government, in the person of the Home Secretary, received the news of the violence at Olympia with indignation and suggestions for anti-fascist legislation. These latter made interesting reading. One of them proposes to prohibit organizations of a military character, and the wearing of a uniform and drilling. Two months after this suggestion was offered to the Opposition parties for their endorsement it was reported that a company had been registered with a capital of £100,000 for the setting up of a corps of uniformed private police to guard the property of those Londoners who care to pay for the service. Reporting this project the *New Statesman and Nation* pointed out that: "Here is another private army in the making, with nothing so far as can be seen to prevent its being captured—by the simple method of undisclosed recruitment into its ranks —by the Mosley fascists, or any other shirted body."

Another proposal submitted by the government was that the authorities should take powers to prohibit large bodies of people marching from outside into a town when such a march threatens disorder. On examination it turns out, first, that such marches, if they cause reasonable men to fear a breach of the peace, are already illegal, and second, that fascists do not indulge in this form of exercise. Unlike hungry unemployed, they can afford to make their excursions by lorry. The uncharitable might regard such proposals as cynical attempts to confuse the public mind as to the real powers of the police

THE WITHDRAWAL OF BRITISH DEMOCRACY 95

in order to allow them greater freedom to ban open-air meetings of unemployed at Labour Exchanges, and to arrest working-class leaders without charge of any offence committed.

The government, however, is not always so tortuous in its attempts to crush its opponents as these little flutters in oppression would seem to imply. Lest the increase of police powers and the insertion of guaranteed gentlemen into the forces should not be sufficient to convince all men of the real nature of the government's intentions, these measures were supported by the decision, announced in Parliament on March 15, 1934, to create a new branch of the Territorial Army, to be called the Royal Defence Corps. This fine body of men will be made up of ex-Regulars and ex-Territorials, to be used in emergency "to protect vulnerable points in this country from any attack by persons of ill-will or foreign agents inside the country," and controlled, unlike other forms of special constabulary, by the central government. This suggestion was met in some quarters by the naïve suggestion that a better method of dealing with "foreign agents" is the one which has proved quite efficient in the past, namely, their subjection to the good offices of the Secret Service. It is feared that those who advance this suggestion are unaware of the fact that the day of Mr. E. Phillips Oppenheim has passed. The chief peacetime danger to the state is no longer the beautiful and titled foreign agent, given to catch-as-catch-can with Kings' Messengers in *trains de luxe*. Since Moscow became a large-scale exporter of gold the distinguishing characteristics of the foreign agent have changed. They may now be known not by their beauty or rank, but by their sympathy with and/or membership of the working class. Therefore, in place of the political police capable of dealing with the first class traveller in ill-will, it is thought that a picked body of veterans is necessary to withstand the mass assaults of a now vulgarized profession.

But sudden attacks upon "vulnerable points" are not the only form of activity to which these enemies of the state are given. In the Standing Committee discussion on the Incitement to Disaffection Bill, a Major Proctor disclosed that "there were men in this country, paid agents of a foreign Power, who not only exploited the poor, but who would destroy, if they could, the I.L.P. and the Labour party in the so-called interests of the poor, but in reality in the interests of the Third International."[1] It is not, therefore, only the emergency of attack that must be met; there is a constant menace in the hard preparatory work of exploitation which these agents put in between attacks. One might assume that the authorities felt this danger could be met in part by a further resort to what may be called the picked-veteran system. One may imagine the idea that something might be done by appointing a Controller of Output at the B.B.C. At all events, the choice fell upon the veteran Colonel

---

[1] For another view, see J. Ramsay MacDonald, *Parliament and Revolution* (1919), where it is argued that "the Russian Revolution has been one of the greatest events in the history of the world, and the attacks that have been made upon it by frightened ruling classes and hostile capitalism should rally to its defence everyone who cares for political liberty and freedom of thought."

Alan Dawnay, formerly of the Coldstream Guards, later First Grade General Staff Officer at the War Office and at all times brother to a director of Vickers, Ltd. The output from foreign agents fell off almost immediately. Mr. Vernon Bartlett was first cautioned and then dropped entirely, Messrs. Ferrie and Staunton were cautioned, and the Hunger Marchers were refused permission to broadcast.

Unfortunately, perhaps, for the National Government, the B.B.C. is not the only medium through which opinion may be expressed. The problem of ill-will is too wide and subtle to be dealt with by ex-soldiers alone. Even the heads of the Services understand the danger of allowing emergencies to develop. They fear, moreover, that even their regular and special veterans may not be proof against seduction. In order, therefore, to make quite sure that the forces of law and order should rest firmly in the hands of the propertied classes, the government put through its Incitement to Disaffection Bill. "Put through" does not perhaps adequately describe the operation. From the point of view of its opponents in the House, "smuggled" might be a more accurate term. It is a convention of the constitution that the law officers of the Crown should, while remaining loyal to the Cabinet, perform the special expert duty of maintaining complete impartiality whenever they explain to the House the legal technicalities of a government Bill. The Attorney-General, however, attempted to "get by" the House of Commons with an assurance that the Bill was a "procedure Bill, rather than in any way altering the substance of our law." Having been granted the second reading for which that assurance was an argument, he disclosed in the Bill a sub-section making it an offence to attempt to do any act preparatory to an offence. This might seem a startling piece of legislation, but, the Attorney-General pointed out, it was in fact no more than a reproduction of a section of the Official Secrets Act which the Liberals had passed. Though perhaps ingenious, the contention was false. The Liberal measure reads "aid or abets and does any act preparatory to," thus making the preparatory act not an offence in itself but a limitation upon aiding and abetting. In the Disaffection Bill the word "or" was substituted for the word "and." In the second reading no one noticed the change, with the result that a House that had been assured that the substance of the law would not be altered was made to participate in the creation of a new offence. In like manner the Bill substituted "duty or allegiance" for the "duty and allegiance" of the Mutiny Act, making it an offence to persuade soldiers not only to mutiny but to disregard even the most trivial of military regulations. Just as in this case the Attorney-General claimed to be merely re-enacting the Mutiny Act, so he maintained that the right of search clause was nothing more than a repetition of the provisions of existing legislation. He denied that it was an illustration of the General Warrant, which it quite clearly is, and he again cited the Official Secrets Acts as analogous, which in view of their more precise wording they as clearly are not. The convention that the law officers of the Crown preserve impartiality has long been regarded as essential to parliamentary government. It is not difficult to see in its handling of the Sedition Bill yet another illustration of the fact that the Government is only concerned with parliamentary forms in the sense that it is prepared to abandon them whenever their observance would impede the operation of reactionary policy.

Nor are parliamentary conventions the only things which are affected by the passage of this Bill. By its provisions those freedoms which a democratic society is accustomed to expect as the normal condition of political controversy are endangered. In Lord Parmoor's words the Bill was "an obvious attempt to drive political controversy within the danger of criminal prosecution."

As first presented Clause 1 of the Bill read: "If any person endeavours to seduce any member of His Majesty's Forces from his duty or allegiance to His Majesty he shall be guilty of an offence under this Act." After protest the clause was amended to read: "If any person maliciously or advisedly endeavours, etc.," which means that the person seducing must know that the object of his attentions is a soldier, and, contrary to the Attorney-General's first suggestion, should not be imprisoned for a crime he did not intend to commit. But a new offence has been created, and, as the *New Statesman and Nation* has pointed out, we have here for the first time a measure which brackets together for similar treatment a member of the Society of Friends, a foreign spy, and the publisher of an obscene libel.

The second clause is an even greater departure from the principles of English law. "If any person, with intent to commit or to aid, abet, counsel or produce the commission of an offence under Section 1 of this Act, has in his possession or under his control any document of such a nature that the dissemination thereof among members of His Majesty's forces would constitute an offence he shall be guilty of an offence under this Act." Under this heading could be included all socialist and pacifist literature. Nor will it be necessary for the prosecution to prove intention to disseminate—a conviction can follow upon simple possession. The result of the Bill will be, and has already been,[1] to hold a constant threat over the heads of both publishers and printers, and to prevent, through the exercise of a private censorship of printers, the publication of material which presumably even the Attorney-General would, at the present moment, be prepared to recognize as legal. Both publishers and printers will be afflicted with the necessity of taking anxious thought against the day when some hysterically patriotic jury will be led to believe that a mild or general statement of pacifism or socialism, published years before, constitutes an incitement to disaffection.

The Act has, therefore, a twofold purpose: first, to provide, in time of crisis, for the destruction of the right of free speech, and, second, to reduce, even in normal times, the volume of literature which seeks to reproduce such seditious teachings as those of Christ or Marx on the subjects of war and poverty.

[1] See a letter to *The Times* of Tuesday, November 6, 1934, signed by Jonathan Cape, Hugh Dent, Geoffrey Faber, George Harrap, Allen Lane, Stanley Unwin, and Leonard Woolf, quoting a case of the refusal of a printer to print pacifist propaganda.

The phrase "with intent to commit," etc., was put in under pressure as an amendment to replace "without lawful excuse." The latter would have put the onus of disproving wrongful intention upon the accused, the former shifts that onus to the prosecution. Even so the sub-section remains as a complete departure from established legal principle. Since Reg. *v.* Eagleton in 1855 the courts have understood that "the mere intention to commit a misdemeanour is not criminal. Some act is required. . . ." But with the passage of this Bill the prosecution does not need to prove that "action" has been taken. Mere "proof" of intention will be sufficient.

Section 11 of Clause 11 of the original Bill made it possible for a person to be sent to prison for doing something that a magistrate believed to be preparatory to committing an offence; for doing something, for example, as wicked as buying a ticket to Aldershot while holding membership in the Communist party. As it happened, the forging of such a dictatorial weapon proved too much even for the 90 per cent totalitarian National Government. The section was dropped in Standing Committee, although the Attorney-General was afraid that its omission would entail "a certain amount of risk."

The third section of the same clause gives an unlimited right of search hitherto prohibited by law. Since Lord Camden's decision in the Wilkes case it has been regarded as a basic English liberty that the police have no right to search persons, places, or premises in the general hope of finding a document which may prove incriminating.

This, reflected the National Government, was all very well, but what was good enough for Mr. Wilkes is not good enough for Mr. Elias. They were prompted to this reflection by the fact that Lord Trenchard, as Police Commissioner, had recently been successfully sued by members of the National Unemployed Workers' movement for trespass and detention of documents by the police on the occasion of a police visitation and search of the offices of the N.U.W.M. on November 1, 1932. They decided that what they could not obtain from Mr. Justice Horridge they would obtain by Act of Parliament. "I do not know of anything worse," says Professor Laski, "than when a decision concerning freedom of the subject has gone against the government the government should then reverse the decision by an Act of Parliament." Equally sinister was the government's original intention, under Section I of Clause III, to deny the elementary right of trial by jury to persons charged with an offence under the Act. Thanks, however, to the protests of the public in general and lawyers in particular, that right was restored. At least, protest may have been the cause of its restoration—one cannot be quite certain. It is of course remotely possible that someone may have reminded Mr. MacDonald that in 1916, when sentences were being given for the possession of seditious documents, he said: "These prosecutions affect the most fundamental liberties of British subjects. . . . I appeal for a fair trial. Prosecute us as much as you like, bring us up as often as you like, ruin us by the expense of defending ourselves, even if we are successful, if you like, but do let us go before the High Court, do let us have a jury. Do let us have an appeal to the House of Lords itself, so that, at any rate, we shall get a decision from a body which is constitutionally minded, and which is not moved in the way these magistrates undoubtedly have been moved."[1]

[1] Mr. MacDonald in a speech in the House of Commons on June 29, 1916.

VI

REACTION—THE NEXT STAGE

THE record of the National Government is largely the history of a movement away from democracy. The tampering with parliamentary forms, the reorganization of the police and their increasing violence, the restrictions upon free speech and assembly, the Royal Defence Corps, the Unemployment Act, and the Incitement to Disaffection Act—behind all these is a purpose essentially fascist. It is often maintained that a political movement which is not accompanied by the psychological and emotional disturbances which characterized Nazi "counter-revolution" cannot appropriately be termed fascist. There is, however, no reason to confuse the more pathological symptoms of the members of a party with the essential character of the movement. There are fewer instances of violence, hysteria, and sadistic cruelty to be found in Italy than in Germany, and no one supposes thereby that Italy is the less fascist. The fascism of Germany, moreover, is marked by anti-semitism, a practice and a habit of mind unknown to the Italian movement. These manifestations of mental distress are not fundamental to fascism. They have no inseparable connection with its essential feature, which is simply the transformation of capitalist democracy into capitalist dictatorship. Whenever there exists a tendency to restrict democratic freedoms as a means of maintaining the hold of property on the power of the state there exists a movement which is essentially fascist.

The National Government, with its slow encroachment upon democracy, may seem to have little in common with the dictatorships of Mussolini or Hitler with their violent annihilation of every liberal principle. Each of these, however, faced in one degree or another with crisis, has found it necessary to follow a common path in exalting the power of the executive, mobilizing public opinion, and departing from the normal procedure of party government. Mr. MacDonald's government has not yet explored its avenues to the point where the power of the executive is exalted into autocratic personal dictatorship, where public opinion is mobilized into a mass fascist movement and where the party system is replaced by the totalitarian state. Mr. Baldwin has said that we shall never reach that point, that "Britain will not stand for a dictatorship from the Right or from the Left." It may be suggested that the growth of fascism in Britain along continental lines does not depend upon Mr. Baldwin's conception of what is and what is not likely to be distasteful to the British political sense. Fascism will develop in spite of Mr. Baldwin's assurances, as it developed in spite of Hindenburg's assurances, when economic decline proceeds to a point where the ownership of power by property is seriously threatened. British capitalism may be reluctant to carry fascism to German lengths, but if private ownership of the means of production and the flow of free income therefrom are menaced, there is nothing in its history to suggest that it will experience great difficulty in putting first things first.

Great Britain has given proof of the enormous reserves

of strength of her economic machine. These reserves, together with policies of restriction, rationalization, economy, currency depreciation, and tariffs have helped to pull Great Britain out of the worst of the depression. The City, like every other creditor, has suffered, but there is reason to believe, with regard to overseas investments, that 1933 was the worst year and that there may soon be an improvement in the rate of income. During the past year the profits of leading industrial companies have been rising. Industrial activity is back at pre-crisis level, exports have risen, and the building, the iron and steel, the aviation, and the motor-car trades achieved a marked degree of recovery.

These evidences of recovery will, however, bear examination. How are they brought about? Much of the improvement has been due to increased rationalization, chiefly to the kind known as "speeding up," with the result that the industrial worker—when in work—is producing approximately 20 per cent more than he did in pre-depression days.[1] Together with currency depreciation, rationalization has been responsible for much of the expansion of British exports which have not, however, risen to even 60 per cent of the 1929 figure. Rationalization means a lowering of the costs of production and an increased opportunity for profits. In the case of the coalfields, for example, "the average output per shift in the first quarter of 1934 was pushed up to 23·32 cwt.,

[1] Colin Clark in the *Economic Journal* of September 1934 notes that since 1929 "the increase in production has been of the order of magnitude of two and a half times the increase in investment."

so that the profit was maintained at over 1s. per ton, though wages fell from 9s. 2d. to 8s. 5d. a shift and production from 60 to 53 million tons."[1] Recovery, under these conditions, means largely recovery in those luxury and semi-luxury trades which cater for the recipients of dividends. In the basic industries and in international trade improvement has been much less marked. Moreover, the fact that the average industrial activity has regained a pre-crisis level is no indication of substantial recovery. For in order to maintain normal conditions a rate of improvement of at least 2 per cent a year is required, and we have not yet begun to make up for the improvement forgone since 1929. Recovery would appear to depend upon the continued maintenance of recent advances and upon improvement in the international economic sphere.

The government seeks to promote the first condition by a protective tariff designed to secure British producers a greater share of the domestic market and by price-raising schemes for increasing home agricultural production. But with rising prices—relative to the prices of other goods—the consumer buys less of the protected commodities. The unusual circumstances of the last two years have made it possible to increase domestic output without a rise in working-class purchasing power, but it is unlikely that further increases in output will be achieved. They could be achieved if prices were kept low in relation to other goods. As it is, imports will continue to be displaced without a corresponding increase in home production. The Argentine, Australia, New

[1] *Labour Research*, August 1934, p. 173

Zealand, Denmark, and the West Indies depend almost entirely upon the British market for the disposal of their produce, and it would seem that, sooner or later, Major Elliot's policies will not only be stultified in the home market but will also produce an adverse effect upon British exports and a fresh decline in the returns from overseas investments.

Other than through the recovery of the world market there is only one way of expanding British output—by an expansion of the market through a reduction in the price charged to the consumer. The protective policy adopted by the National Government amounts virtually to a guarantee that prices will not be reduced. For in no case has protection been made conditional upon increased efficiency in production or distribution. The government has turned a deaf ear to the protests against the rising prices of agricultural commodities. And the iron and steel trades have—as a condition prerequisite of protection—produced a scheme of reorganization of which it may be said that the cynicism brought to its formulation is equalled only by the cynicism with which it is regarded by those who are supposed to believe in it.

The circumstances of the depression and the fact that Britain was in 1929 less well equipped than many other countries with weapons of economic warfare have made it possible for a discriminative tariff to bring about an increase in British industrial production for home consumption. The iron and steel, the coal, the motor-car, the aviation, and the building trades have all been recently showing increased profits, largely as the result of drastic reductions in manufactured imports. And, with the

REACTION—THE NEXT STAGE 109

expansion of the home output, the imports of raw materials have increased considerably since 1931. At the end of 1934, however, both imports of raw materials and the volume of British industrial production have shown reductions sufficiently marked to suggest the possibility of a slowing down in the rate of industrial improvement. It is possible that the domestic producer has already reached the limits of a domestic market which tariffs and quotas can reallocate but not expand.

The achievement of recovery depends, for Major Elliot, upon the fulfilment of the first condition mentioned above —the maintenance of recent advances in the domestic sphere. His efforts towards self-sufficiency appear to be based upon a pessimistic view of the future of international trade. He is impressed with the fact that when our exports, visible and invisible, have paid for our imports, there is, as in 1931, nothing left over for fresh investment overseas, that the prices of our imports are likely to rise further than those of our exports, and that even a slight improvement in industry and consequently of the purchasing power of those at present unemployed will mean an increased demand for foodstuffs. Hence the quotas, subsidies, and marketing schemes. It has already been suggested that these methods are peculiar in that they are an attempt, first, to increase home consumption of domestic products by raising prices, and second, to meet a future increased demand for foodstuffs by a limitation of imports that can only react adversely upon British exports and revenue from foreign investments. At this point, however, the peculiarities of the Minister's special brand of national self-sufficiency are of less importance than the fact of his choice of the path of self-sufficiency. For implicit in that choice is the conviction that no recovery in world trade would allow British exports to expand sufficiently to enable us to finance an increased demand for foodstuffs. It is not that Major Elliot has abandoned the hope of world recovery, he has merely abandoned the hope that such a recovery would be of any real assistance to the British export trade.

It is not difficult to find good reasons for his pessimism. The cotton trade is our largest exporting industry, accounting for more than a fifth of our total exports. But no one has any faith in the ability of the cotton trade to retain its present markets, much less recover those it has lost. The coal trade is faced with the development of economies in fuel, and with ever-increasing competition from foreign mines and from every alternative source of power. The iron and steel trades have obtained command of the home market, but they will have to pay the price of protection by meeting the intensified competition in export markets from German, French, and Belgian products which can no longer be sold in Britain. The future for exports of machinery is brighter, but the woollen industry, which is next in importance, faces high tariffs in almost every foreign market. It would seem that the trades which account for approximately half the value of British exports have little or nothing to hope for from a restoration of world economic activity. The National Government has done what it can for them with tariffs, quotas, and currency depreciation. But this protectionist policy seems to have reached the limits of its efficacy as a method of consoling the export trades for the loss of foreign markets by providing benefits in the home market. Manufactured imports have already been drastically cut down and there are obvious dangers in further reductions of food imports. Moreover, the government's measures have already produced tariff reprisals abroad and an increasing cost of living at home. Further instalments of protection can only arouse working-class feeling at home and provoke violent reactions abroad.

The certain decline of the strength of British capitalism, relatively to that of its younger rivals, may well be a long drawn-out process. Britain has vast reserves of strength, as was shown by the fact that she has only recently been forced to pick up weapons of economic warfare which other states have been using for years. Those reserves enabled her to avoid the worst effects of depression. But they were built up largely out of the export trades—trades which are now showing themselves less and less able to meet foreign competition. Decline *may* be long drawn out; on the other hand America may rapidly reassume the position of pre-crisis days, and it is significant that while in the United Kingdom industrial production was reported in November 1934 as slightly above the 1927–9 level, in Japan it has risen 40 per cent.

Sooner or later economic rivalry will develop to the point of acute crisis. The property-owning classes of Great Britain will be brought face to face with the choice between acquiescence in a further and fatal period of erosion of the power of British capitalism and the taking of some form of drastic remedial action. And when that point has been reached there will be present in Britain the basic condition of fascism. In crisis capitalism will make desperate attempts to maintain itself. The acquisition of markets wherein British enterprise can operate undisturbed by stronger rivals will become imperative. Some markets have, in fact, already been discovered. Indeed, British capitalism is never likely to suffer decline without a struggle so long as Lord Beaverbrook owns a newspaper. It has for some time been possible, at the cost of 1d., to become acquainted with the only policy which can stay the breakdown of the British economic machine. The noble lord's personal attacks on Mr. Baldwin may cause his circulation figures temporarily to decline. But the main burden of his message will sooner or later be recognized as the obvious policy for a distressed capitalism anxious for survival. At that moment property will decide that Ottawa is not enough, that the White paper is too much, and that the future is not with the mildness and caution of Mr. Baldwin. Crisis will do what Lord Beaverbrook has so far been unable to do, even with the help of Mr. Churchill and Lord Salisbury—it will convince the Conservative party of the urgent necessity of Empire Free Trade. In distress, British capitalism will not refuse the promise of monopolistic advantage contained in that policy. It will plunge into the reorganization of the Empire as a vast market to be preserved for the sole use of British industrialists, gazing meanwhile upon horizons that have been dark since the 'seventies. The Conservative Central Office may have the great economic reserves of Britain behind it, but time is on the side of the *Daily Express*.

In a future crisis it is probable also that the same

domestic policy will be pursued as that which gave so much relief to property in 1931—as in that year we shall meet future emergency not only with tariffs but with economy as well. Profit will demand that as little as possible shall be spent upon wages and social services. A more severe onslaught will be made upon working-class and middle-class standards of living.

It may be that these external and internal remedies can be applied without arousing great opposition, and in that case capitalist reaction will be achieved without resort to fascism. If, on the other hand, the policies of economy and tariffs are seriously challenged it will be possible to solve the deadlock in only one way. If capitalism, desperately in need of relief, finds the execution of its remedial policies blocked, it will take steps to crush those responsible for the obstruction.

Clearly the factor of opposition will be operative in Britain if a severe crisis leads to the adoption of reactionary measures. The period of depression and decline preceding actual crisis will have brought steadily worsening conditions for the working class. As a climax will come, first, the transition to Empire Free Trade with its expulsion from Great Britain of foreign foodstuffs and raw materials, and, second, the wholesale reductions in wages and social services as a result of some new banker's decision that the pound is in danger. An already high cost of living would, therefore, be greatly increased at the moment when purchasing power was being reduced.

Opposition would come, in the first place, from the trade unions. Through the Labour party which they dominate, and through industrial action, every effort would be made to avoid wage reductions, particularly in the sheltered and highly organized industries, and to combat in Parliament proposals for reducing the amount spent on social services. It is true that the trade unions are not primarily socialist, that they are, rather, a powerful vested interest within capitalism which expands or contracts with the welfare or decline of capitalism. They do not, however, appreciate the implications of their position sufficiently to recognize the moment for contraction when it arrives. They will explain away a wage cut as industrially necessary—after the cut has been made. They will not make reductions of their own accord. For, while many of their leaders suspect that wages are a cost of production to be lowered in lean times, many of the rank and file are concerned less with the economics of capitalism than with high wages. The history of the Labour party suggests that it will oppose any demands for reduced individual or social income made as a result of deepening crisis.

In the second place opposition will come from organizations, within or without the Labour party, which are determined upon the realization of socialism. The present emphasis in British socialist circles is upon a legalism and constitutionalism that not only proscribes the Communist party and all its works, but also sees nothing but mischief in the attempts of such organizations as the Socialist League to formulate a socialist policy which seeks to make of democratic institutions tools to be used rather than idols to be worshipped. But in the event of a fresh drift towards depression, the movement away from "democracy at any price" may begin to assume the proportions of a serious opposition, intent, like the trade unions, upon maintaining wages, but also intent upon the carrying out of a large-scale programme of socialism.

Neither form of opposition, reformist or socialist, can be tolerated by a distressed capitalism. In office, the working-class movement threatens disaster via taxation or nationalization. Out of office it stands in the way of capitalist "reorganization." And at the moment when the champions of property decide that in deepening crisis such opposition is fatal to the maintenance of capitalism the day of British fascism will have dawned. For it will no longer be sufficient to rely on financial panics to set up Coalition Governments, to be content with a "constitutional" movement away from democracy. It will be necessary to prepare for a much more serious situation, to make dispositions for the crushing of working-class organizations and for the abolition of democratic forms and institutions—for the annihilation of everything which stands in the way of capitalist survival.

If the mere matter of Ulster could lead to the virtual abandonment of the parliamentary method, the defiance of democratic principle, the organization of a private army and disloyalty to a popularly elected government on the part of the Army, it is not improbable that a more serious crisis for the British bourgeoisie will give rise to more strenuous efforts towards reaction. The constitution is no less "unwritten" and flexible than it was in 1914, and if the ruling class had no qualms about twisting it to defeat Liberals they are unlikely to hesitate when the issue is that of capitalist survival. Already the right wing of the Conservative party expresses openly its contempt for democratic institutions. Will it not one day be tempted to do for the Empire as a whole what it now seeks to do for India? Sir Edward Carson and Mr. F. E. Smith could not resist the fascination of the private army; can we be sure that Mr. Winston Churchill, with his fondness for parading the military, and Lord Lloyd, with his strenuous imperialism, will remain inactive when the call comes to defend the foundations of British society? With Lord Beaverbrook, Lord Rothermere, Mr. Amery, and others, do they not form a potential fascist leadership to which a harassed capitalism might well turn for guidance out of the wilderness of foreign competition, working-class demands, and democratic delays? Given Hitler's 51·7 per cent of the votes cast in a hysterical election, will such leaders be backward in proscribing the Opposition, imprisoning its leaders, and setting up a complete dictatorship?

As the potential leading spirits of a fascist movement, the diehards are perhaps more dangerous than Sir Oswald Mosley and his British Union of Fascists. Certainly Mr. Churchill and his associates have an advantage in that they are already in the public mind as statesmen of experience, whereas Sir Oswald Mosley is known to be experienced in almost everything except the business of statesmanship. And while highly coloured and even spectroscopic political records may count against certain of the diehards, in any future bid for public support they will be far less handicapped thereby than will Sir Oswald, by popular recollection of his habit of sloughing, with almost reptilian facility, any distinguishing marks and restrictive bonds which might interfere with his political development.

The Tory Right Wing may decide to stand independently as claimants for fascist honours. On the other hand they may choose to join forces with the British Union of Fascists and to avail themselves of a well-organized if small private army. It remains to be seen in what hands the leadership of fascism in Britain will finally rest. In the meantime it is worth while to reflect upon the development of the private fascist army in Britain, noting that while the British Union of Fascists may not be the final form of organization which will succeed in Britain, it has successfully established itself in competition with other fascist bodies.

These earlier organizations, such as the British Fascisti and the United Empire Fascist party, have never deserved and have never received any support or even attention from the British public. Anti-semitic, intensely patriotic, highly irresponsible, and embarrassingly adolescent, they were, even in their best days between 1923 and Mosley's fascist début in 1932, never able to count on a combined membership of more than a few thousand. Their leaders were drawn either from the class of retired military officers, as in the case of Brigadier-General R. B. D. Blakeney and Rear-Admiral J. C. Armstrong of the British Fascisti, or from that shadowy class of persons such as Mr. A. S. Leese, the "Director-General" of the Imperial Fascist League, Mr. Serocold Skeels of the United Empire Fascist party, which competes with the Group movement for the attention of the undergraduate, and Mr. Gilmour, ex-propagandist of the Independent

Labour party—later editor of the journal of the Scottish Fascist Democratic party—persons who have unaccountably strayed from their rightful fold which is the local headquarters of the Conservative party.

Void of experience in political matters, ignorant of the real meaning and purpose of fascism, such of these organizations as were still in existence in 1932 lost most of their membership to the newly formed British Union of Fascists. The latter started with the advantage of a leader who undoubtedly knew what he wanted, having arrived at fascism by a process of elimination, after a rapid sampling of whatever goods the other parties had to offer. Beginning as a Conservative Member of Parliament he was regarded as a young man of great promise. He is said to have been assured an eventual place in the Cabinet—given patience and hard work. Perhaps there were other reasons than a lack of patience and industry; perhaps even the assurance was never given; however that may be, he became first an Independent and then, in 1923, a member of the Labour party. The standards of patience and industry required by the Labour party are not, it seems, inflexible in the case of wealthy young men anxious to win to positions of commanding importance. Within three years of joining, Sir Oswald was elected to the Labour party executive, and in the following year, 1928, was re-elected, on each occasion securing a very large vote. At the formation of the Labour government in 1929 Mr. J. H. Thomas was appointed Minister in charge of Unemployment and Mosley became his assistant. A year later unemployment had increased rapidly, and Mosley had seen all his work-finding schemes rejected by the Treasury and by Mr. Thomas. Resignation from the government followed, together with efforts to win a parliamentary backing for his proposals as outlined in the Mosley Memorandum. But public works and pensions schemes in the Rooseveltian manner proved unattractive to the large majority of Labour M.PS, and, for the seventeen faithful, there was little else to do beyond the issuing in November 1930 of a Manifesto or programme of national reconstruction. Convinced of the impossibility of winning support for such a programme from the Labour party, or indeed any other, Mosley and seven supporters—six Labour and one Conservative—formed the New party, with a policy of national planning and an appeal to patriotic lovers of action.

It may be that Mosley never hoped to win widespread electoral support for the policy of planning and social compromise as proclaimed by the New party. In any case, the result of the Ashton-under-Lyne by-election of 1931 demonstrated clearly that if he waited for the electoral success of the New party to ensure the carrying out of his policy he would wait for ever. Mr. John Strachey, who accompanied Mosley in his wanderings into but not beyond the New party, asserts that this was not the only thing demonstrated by the Ashton experience. In his *Menace of Fascism* he writes: "The result of the election had just been announced and it was seen that the intervention of the New party had defeated the Labour candidate and elected the Conservative. The crowd consisted of most of the keenest workers in all the neighbouring Lancashire towns . . . the crowd was violently hostile to Mosley and the New party. It roared at him, and, as he stood facing it, he said to me, 'That is the crowd that has prevented anyone doing anything in England since the war.' At that moment British fascism was born. At that moment of passion, and some personal danger, Mosley found himself almost symbolically aligned against the workers. He had realized in action that his programme could only be carried out after the crushing of the workers and their organizations."[1]

From Ashton until the General Election of the same year Mosley spoke increasingly in fascist terms, eventually deciding that what he meant by social compromise and national reconstruction was the corporate state, and that there could be no corporate state without a private army. At the end of 1931, therefore, the final step was taken and the scanty debris of the New party became the British Union of Fascists. Having thus at last completed the search for political truth, Mosley was able to turn his whole attention to its proclamation. Hence *Greater Britain* with its formal statement of fascist policy. In this work Mosley introduces us to the secrets of capitalism without tears. It appears that under the corporate state Britain will enjoy all those advantages which fascism in Germany and Italy promised but never provided. Class war will be replaced by national co-operation. "All who pursue a sectional and anti-national policy will be opposed by the might of the organized state." Everyone is catered for. "Profit can be made, provided that the activity enriches the nation as well as the individual." While as for labour: "Corporations of

[1] *The Menace of Fascism*, p. 161

self-governing areas of industry . . . will be charged with the task of raising wages and salaries." The Fascist government will have "absolute power of action" subject to "the power of Parliament to dismiss it by vote of censure"—after Parliament has been re-formed. The franchise is to be occupational and the House of Lords automatically superseded by the "National Corporation" or Parliament of Industry. Within this body the trade unions will perform their purely consultative functions. Arbitration will be compulsory, and, like prices and investments, wages will be "regulated."

Having thus established the corporate state, Mosley outlines its policy in the economic and political spheres, and, significantly enough, his programme for the salvation of Britain is substantially the same as that of the Tory reactionaries. Where they demand Empire Free Trade, he intends to introduce "scientific protection," to "radically overhaul our system of defence," and to fortify "islands on the Cape route to India."

More original than his economics of imperialism is his description of the means by which fascism will rise to power. At one moment he promises strict adherence to constitutional forms, and asks only for the opportunity peacefully to obtain a majority at the polls. At another he states that "by one road or another we are determined that fascism shall come to Britain." If the democratic method allows him to succeed, there will presumably be no violence, but if he is opposed, if "every appeal to reason is futile in the future, as it has been in the immediate past," then we are to expect the use of force and the establishment of dictatorship.

In the exploration of "one road or another" much has been learnt from Nazi pathfinders who have demonstrated the effectiveness of certain kinds of propaganda providing easy access to public opinion. For example, in the belief that nothing succeeds like success, every effort is made to create a general impression that the British Union is larger and more powerful than it actually is. Emphasis is laid on the heroic destiny of youth and the tragic failure of the "old men." The whole movement is marked by that romantic anti-rational attitude which proved so attractive in Germany, and which may, even allowing for differences in national temperament, make many converts in Britain among those anxious for a change of emotional climate. Like Hitler, Mosley seems to be aware that his fundamental task is to get himself established in the public eye as the enemy of all that is intellectual, and if he is successful in removing politics and economics from the realm of ideas into the realm of "feeling" and "honour" in the German manner, it does not greatly matter, as it did not matter with Hitler, if the actual programme of the party is a confused mass of indiscriminate and contradictory proposals. For those to whom fascism appeals are concerned less with where they are going than with the pleasurable sensations of movement. These are provided in Britain by the *Blackshirt* and the *Fascist Week*, with their rabid coursing after every middle-class grievance; by the military terminology with its "G.H.Q.," "Chief of Staff" and "Intelligence Officer"; by occasional spells of "active service" at evictions, strikes, and tithe disputes; and by the theatrical mass meetings with their opportunities for posturing and violence.

If, like the Boy Scout movement, the B.U.F. sought merely to relieve street-corner boredom, the movement might financially be self-supporting. But the Blackshirt with his social grievances is a worse case than the elementary school boy with his empty evenings, and requires, for his distraction, not only uniforms and bands, but also large halls, spot lights, lorries, armoured cars, and weekly payments for propaganda services rendered. On the one hand it is clear that organizations like the B.U.F. are an extremely expensive undertaking, on the other that Mosley's private fortune is not unlimited. We may conclude, therefore, with a government spokesman that: "The exact source from which income is derived to finance these activities is unknown, but it is obvious that substantial financial backing is forthcoming from various sources other than that of the private wealth of the leader and the dues or subscriptions of members."[1]

As little is known of the size and rate of growth of the movement as of the source of its financial supplies. At the beginning of 1934, various newspapers "on good authority" estimated the membership at anything from 17,000 to 500,000. Certainly it was not large enough to allow Lord Rothermere to declare for fascism and at the same time to maintain the general popularity of the Rothermere Press. The probability is that the membership is not much more than 100,000 and that while the movement is gaining ground, it is doing so very slowly.

Public opinion may well refuse to be impressed by such small-scale swashbuckling. And, certainly, in the existing political and economic conditions the possibilities

[1] Lord Feversham, in the House of Lords, February 28, 1934.

of fascist expansion appear to be limited. Nevertheless, a beginning has been made. No one, moreover, can guarantee the continued existence of present conditions. The one thing certain is that a period of decline, with increasing economic distress and political dissatisfaction, will produce an enormous increase in the numbers of those susceptible to the fascist appeal.

Even to-day half the electorate of Britain is, virtually, indifferent to the old parties. Much of that indifference can be traced to those members of the lower and middle classes whose habit of mind is to avoid all unnecessary contact with everyday life. Questions of politics and economics are largely without meaning to those who have been put to work at the age of fourteen, after perhaps ten years of elementary school education. Their sources of information about public affairs are the highly coloured and dramatically simplified accounts given by a popular press which exploits for profit their emotional dissatisfactions. Before the war the public-house, the race-track, and the music-hall sufficed. But with the new elementary education, with the influx of women into business, and with the application of inventiveness to the entertainment industry, beer, betting, and variety, as doors to a brighter world, have been supplemented by the cinema, the two-penny library, the cheap magazine, and Saturday football. As Mr. Hemingway has pointed out, religion is by no means the only opium of the people.

Here, among the readers of the *Mail*, the *Mirror*, the *Sketch*, and the *Express*, are thousands of potential recruits for fascism. Denied employment and the price of distraction, they will be, in their ignorance and irritation, easy prey for fascist propaganda with its skilful manipulation of emotions and its promise of better times.

Among those indifferent to the old parties are many who are more interested in changing their environment than in forgetting it. The majority of these are young enough to be unable to remember the pre-war days when the party system functioned effectively. They lack faith not only in the old parties but in the parliamentary process as well, and, since in their formative years they have seen the futilities of the post-war liberal creeds, they are only to be satisfied by an organization which moves in a determined and convincing manner towards the achievement of "progressive" ends. Programmes of "action" and the reconstruction of Britain on efficient lines have an especial appeal for them. Their German counterparts were won over to fascism without difficulty. Given the circumstances of crisis there is no reason to suppose that the same well-tried methods of propaganda would not be equally successful in Britain.

From his devotion of time and energy to the conversion of the industrial areas it is clear that Mosley looks on economic distress as a certain provider of recruits. It may be that working-class suffering is not yet acute enough in Britain to drive men to desperate ventures, but with continued and worsening depression there will be more and more of the twenty million inhabitants of the distressed areas willing to give him a sympathetic hearing.

There will, of course, be little headway made among the highly skilled, highly organized workers, at least while they retain their faith in the power of reformism to improve or maintain their standards of living. That faith is, however, bound to weaken as mass production, with its rejection of highly skilled labour, weakens trade unions. And over the great part of industrial Britain there is growing disillusionment among erstwhile labour supporters. The unemployed who have lost union protection, and the unskilled, who never had very much, are beginning to believe that in the matter of wages and concessions there is little that labour can do for them. And it may not be long before they, in company with the majority of unorganized British workers, begin to compare and contrast trade unions with corporations, reformism with fascism. They will want to know the difference between the organized capitalism of the public corporations of Mr. Morrison and the national planning and reconstruction of Sir Oswald Mosley. They will begin to wonder as to the comparative advantages of a system of great trade unions representing a powerful vested interest within the capitalist state which increases or decreases with the prosperity or depression of capitalism, and the regular fascist "system," with labour promised its proper "chartered" position within the corporate state. In answering their queries Mosley may point out that a reformism which must observe the rules of capitalist fluctuation is inferior to the brave new party which guarantees unconditional benefits to every worker, skilled or unskilled. It is an answer which will win him many recruits.

It will make its appeal not only to those of the working class who feel themselves both economically disinherited and politically uncared for; in a further period of decline there will also be many black-coated workers with a similar outlook. Already among the organized workers of this class, the civil servants, Post Office workers and teachers, dismay at the effects of the crisis goes hand in hand with disillusionment with the Labour party. Their margin of safety is always slighter than that of those below or above them in the social scale, since they seek to maintain middle-class standards on what is little more than working-class income. And since the war their cost of living and their salaries have tended to move in opposite directions. They have not found Labour governments any more willing than Conservative to relieve their worsening economic position. Like the highly organized German clerical workers, they are apt to feel neglected in a party dominated by the unions of the skilled manual worker. And, like their German counterparts, they may come to feel the attraction of a movement which puts the interest of the lower-middle class in the forefront of its programme.

Such a bait will be even more attractive to the unorganized majority of the clerical workers, most of whom have never enjoyed the sensation of being cared for politically, having always held too firmly to middle-class values to be able to achieve anything so proletarian as trade union solidarity. They are the least politically conscious section of the community. Many of them habitually do not vote, but they can be stampeded in large numbers to the polls by a well-staged panic election. Although their economic status is virtually proletarian, although their experience of depression, with salary cuts and unemployment, has been as bitter as that of the industrial worker, their social outlook remains unfailingly middle class. Exposed to a combination of "forgotten man" propaganda and deepening crisis they could be swept by thousands into the fascist camp.

With the clerks and shop-assistants will go the small traders and shopkeepers and craftsmen, and for similar reasons. Tied, in the industrial areas, to the fortunes of the working class, they have been ruined in large numbers by the depression. And whenever, outside the industrial areas, retail trading shows a profit they are attacked by the large concerns with their cheap mass-produced goods. On the one hand the small man sees his certain extinction in the advance of large-scale industry, department-stores, and multiple shops, on the other he is hostile to and envious of the organized workers with their threat of socialism, and their disciplined demands for increased wages and social services, and their successful co-operative societies. He fears that at the hands of either element he will lose his status as a small capitalist, become declassed, and, as a propertyless man, be forced to take, if he can find it, a working-class job. Fascism plays upon such fears and holds out the hope of a small society of small-scale businesses, a Utopia where the cartels cease from troubling and the unions are suppressed. And when depression sharpens those fears into terror, when uncertainty turns hope into passionate longing, the British petit-bourgeoisie, like the German, will give its vote to fascism.

Within that loose collection of intermediate social strata called the middle class there is a third group capable, in favourable circumstances, of producing good fascist material. The real middle class, the professional men, the managers, and the technicians have, like the clerks and small men, come to know the meaning of economic insecurity. The rising generation finds the professions over-stocked and monopolistic business in need of fewer and fewer technicians, while, with the decline of overseas trade and investment, the number of foreign and colonial posts grows smaller and smaller. When they leave their technical schools and universities they find that they must either live on their families or take themselves, minus training and qualifications, to the Labour Exchange. Those already established find that crisis has dealt severe blows both at their salaries and at their income from investments. Because they live both by work and by ownership they are for the most part politically bewildered and incoherent. As workers they resent salary cuts, while as investors they oppose any attempt to reduce the claims of capital upon industry. They are, in fact, unwilling to accept any idea of conflict between work and ownership. But they are convinced that if the world could be managed by scientists there would be no more disorders and depressions. More than any other class in society thay are, therefore, susceptible to the charm of schemes of capitalist planning. They are attracted by such proposals as the Douglas Credit Scheme because they welcome the idea of an ingenious set of devices that will cure depression and restore capitalism to permanent health without cutting wages, salaries, or interest, without any reference to class conflict. Scientifically the Douglas Credit Scheme has the appearance of what technicians call a "neat job." Economically, it promises the miracle that capitalism in crisis has never yet been able to perform. And as Mr. Louis Anderson Fenn says: "From the psychological point of view Douglasism is an obvious 'defence mechanism' of the middle-class intellectual. It enables him to face the fact that something is wrong with society, without the spiritual disintegration of facing at the same time the prospect of terrifying innovations in his own way of life. 'Blaming the Banker' is in fact the economic correlative of 'original sin' in some kinds of theology. It permits one to face an unpleasant situation without the obligation to do unpleasant things."[1]

But the idea of currency reform, while of great comfort to the middle-class intellectual, lacks that many-sided appeal upon which successful political movements are based. Fascism, with its organized party and with its more colourful and more easily comprehensible remedies, has greater attractions. It knows how to take advantage of every kind of economic discontent and political disillusionment, putting forward special remedies to ease the situation of each separate section of society. To professional men and technicians, therefore, the fascists promise not only the abolition of monopoly and the regimentation of labour, but also such extra suggestions as the dismissal of Jews and the creation of new posts for the faithful through an aggressive imperialist policy.

In the fascist programme there is an appeal to almost every element in society. At present the number of those of the middle class and of the working class who fee that fascism is the solution to their difficulties is small.

[1] *What of the Professional Classes?* p. 8.

But interest in and sympathy with the movement is growing. And what now is largely without interest to clerk and shopkeeper and engineer will take on a new meaning as British capitalism sets off once more towards crisis. The attractions of fascism with its simple handling of complex problems will become more obvious with the growth of poverty, insecurity, and bewilderment, until in a short time demagogy, preaching activism, will have built up a mass movement large enough to attract the interest and financial assistance of those who feel that the carrying out of the reaction necessary for the maintenance of British capitalism calls for a mercenary army. The inspiration and the launching of the B.U.F. will have been due to Mosley, and not the Federation of British Industries; its rank and file from secondary and minor public schools rather than from Eton. But whatever its origins, wherever its members think they are going, its real destiny, if it has one, is to be taken over by industrialists and aristocrats and used to stave off the breakdown of British capitalism. It is clear from a survey of the nature and extent of its activities that the B.U.F. is being secretly subsidized by persons of wealth. Who they are remains a mystery. In the meantime it is important to note other ways besides the financial in which the forces of the Right are coming to look upon Mosley with a more kindly eye. There is no need to make too much of the fact that after the disgusting scenes at Olympia several Conservatives maintained that the Blackshirts had not been excessively brutal and that they were only meting out justice to "Red" interruptors. Nor are Lord Rothermere's spasmodic enthusiasms of much political consequence. But with the "January Club," established to provide a "platform for leaders of fascism and corporate state thought," it appears that, like the Nazis, the British fascists have managed to obtain what Mr. Brailsford calls "a decorative fringe of aristocratic patrons."

With the *English Review* making much of Sir Oswald, and Lady Houston frantically inscribing his virtues in the *Saturday Review*, the Blackshirts may be said also to have their journalistic fringe. More significant is the fact that Lord Lloyd has informed the government that one result of its surrender policy in India will be that "more and more people in this country are likely to prefer a black shirt to a White paper." But the recent rise of Sir Oswald has not been due, except in very small degree, to the diehard element. It has rather been brought about by the Conservative fear that an increasing number of people are likely to prefer a Labour Government to a Tory at the next election. Nothing was thought and little was said of Sir Oswald and his Blackshirts during the first two years after a panic-stricken electorate had given reaction the free hand it needed. British fascism was of no political significance, while the National Government, secure in its huge majority, proceeded with arrogance to carry out a High Tory programme of relieving property at the expense of the poor.

But by 1934 the arrogance began to wear a trifle thin. Conservatism began to doubt whether its budget, tariff, and unemployment policies were the surest road to popularity. The doubts became fears as the Labour party began to win one by-election after another. In local government also substantial labour gains were made, notably in the case of the L.C.C., which for the first time had a labour majority. Nor was the new temper of their opponents calculated to reassure the Tories. The crushing defeat of 1931 had shaken labour faith in gradualism and revived interest in half-forgotten socialist ideas such as nationalization. The Left Wing of the party even went so far as to urge that a government which proposed to embark upon a programme of socialism would need seriously to consider the implications of Conservative resistance in general and of the House of Lords in particular. These developments were viewed by the Right with growing alarm. The arrogance of the National Government has vanished with the reversal of public opinion. The thought of a "socialist dictatorship," with its time divided between confiscating property, abolishing the House of Lords, and criticizing Buckingham Palace, terrifies those who believe that the Socialist League and the party executive are one and the same body. While a conservatism of a less instructed sort is seriously alarmed at the complete lack of harmony between Labour's legislative programme and the needs of property within a depressed capitalism.

It is largely in this setting of Tory apprehension that Mosley has asquired his recent prominence. And it is difficult to see anything in the immediate future of British politics except fresh reason for such apprehension. The Labour Government may not win a clear majority at the election of 1935 or 1936, but it is certain to win many seats and perhaps to arrive by, say, 1938 in the position where it can force a dissolution upon a Conservative Government. If it chooses to do this and to approach the electorate with a Socialist programme and a determined manner, it may well find itself in office with a real majority.

When that happens, Sir Oswald Mosley and the B.U.F. will rise by leaps and bounds in Tory estimation. Whatever labour does, whether it chooses to repeat the tragedy of its last term of office or to move resolutely towards socialism, the result will be a growth in the numbers and political importance of the Blackshirts. For if labour slips back into the opportunism of its last government, many of its supporters will be drawn by disillusionment and disgust and the promise of action into the fascist ranks. At the same time the Right, convinced as always of the inability of labour to administer capitalism without bankrupting it, will see in the growing fascist movement a heaven-sent ally. For with its assistance the Right will be able to repeat the massacre of 1931, when a Labour Cabinet left office rather than make economy cuts, and the electorate was stampeded by the threat of financial catastrophe. A government composed of the more conservative elements in the trade unions and the Co-operative movement, and adamant in its determination to do nothing unconstitutional, can be threatened not only by the bankers with financial disaster but also by the fascists with civil disorder. A Labour Government which adopts self-denying ordinances, ruling out the use of emergency powers of any kind, will give Sir Oswald the opportunity to put on the mantle of Carson and to parade before conservatism as the man who will save the

Empire by hoisting the trade unions with the petard of 1926.

But if, on the other hand, the next Labour Government makes clear its intention of pressing forward with a programme of socialism, Mosley's stock will rise even higher. The situation will be infinitely more critical than that which might be precipitated by any confusion between democratic means and socialist ends. On one side will be arrayed the popularly elected "First Workers' Government," prepared to complete substantial instalments of socialism even if it involves the taking of emergency powers and the abolition of the House of Lords. On the other side will stand the whole class of industrialists, financiers, and landowners who see in the socialist programme a warrant for the annexation of their dominions.

The history of menaced ruling classes in general, and of the British ruling class in 1914 and 1931 in particular, suggests that conservatism will make very determined efforts to prevent the carrying out of socialist plans. But if the Conservative party is in the minority in the House of Commons, and the House of Lords under threat of abolition, the Right will have lost interest in constitutional procedure. Such a situation will give Mosley exactly the opportunity he desires—the opportunity to get himself accepted as the champion of British capitalism by a conservatism more than ready to appreciate the virtues of an organization that is prepared to use any means to achieve its end. And once those virtues are appreciated, once the necessity of shifting the centre of opposition from the parliamentary Conservative party to the B.U.F.

is recognized, Mosley's day will have dawned. For he will then be in full possession of that support from the owners of economic power without which no fascist leader can come to power in Britain or in any other country.

INDEX

Africa, 40, 58
Agricultural Marketing Acts, 54
Air Force, 58
Amery, Mr., 116
Argentine, 40, 42, 107
Armstrong Whitworth, 48
Ashton-under-Lyne, 119
Association of Education Committees, 67
Australia, 54, 58, 107
Austria, 14, 35, 39, 40, 92

Baldwin, Stanley, 35, 47, 58, 105, 112
Bank of Paris, 27
Bartlett, Vernon, 97
Beaverbrook, Lord, 54, 71, 112, 116
Bentham, 75
Bergbauverein Essen, 33
Black-coated Workers, 30, 126
Blackshirt, 122
Blomberg, General von, 37
Board of Education, 63, 68, 69
Boer War, 40
Bose, 37
Brailsford, H. N., 91, 132
Brazil, 42, 54
British Broadcasting Corporation, 96, 97
British Draft, 56
British Empire, 52-54, 116, 135
British Fascisti, 117
British Medical Association, 65

British Union of Fascists, 116, 117, 118, 120, 122, 123, 131-136
Brown Army, 35 ff.
Bruening, 15
Butler, Wm. Harold, 54

Cabinet, 81, 85, 86, 88 ff.
Cabinet Responsibility, 90
Camden, Joseph, 20, 51, 70
Camden, Lord, 101
Canada, 42, 54
Caporetto, 15
Carson, Sir Edward, 116, 134
Central Electricity Board, 80
Ceylon, 49
Chamberlain, Joseph, 23, 51
Chamberlain, Neville, 44, 50, 51, 53
Chili, 42
Churchill, Winston, 116
Circular 1421, 21, 66
Civil Servants, 127
Clerical Workers, 127-130
Coalition Government, 86, 87
Colin Clark, 46, 106
Collective Security, 26, 56, 58
Comité des Forges, 27
Communism, 31
Communist Party, 31, 28, 101, 114
Conservative Party, 112, 116, 132 ff.
Controller of Output, 96
Co-operative Movement, 71, 72, 134

Co-partnership, 80
Corporate State, 30, 33, 35, 120, 121, 126
Covenant of the League, 56, 57
Crown, 91, 97, 98
Crown Colonies, 52

Daily Express, 112, 124
Dawnay, Colonel Alan, 97
Defence of the Realm Act, 87
Delegated Legislation, 91
Denmark, 54, 108
Department Stores, 128
Diehards, 116, 132
Doctor's Mandate, 71
Dominions, 52, 54
Douglas Credit Scheme, 129
Dover, Cliffs of, 59
Dutch East Indies, 49

Economist, 49, 50
Education, 66 ff.
Elliott, Major, 58, 108–110
Emergency Powers Act, 92
Empire Defence Conferences, 58
Empire Free Trade, 112, 113, 121
English Review, 132
"Equilibrium Analysis," 18
Ernst, 37
Ex-officers, 30, 32

Fabian Socialism, 78
Far East, 58
Farmers, 30, 32, 35
Fascist Programmes, 31 ff.
Fascist Week, 122

Feder, Gottfried, 32, 38
Federation of British Industries, 27, 57, 131
Federation of German Industries, 33
Fenn, Louis Anderson, 130
Feversham, Lord, 123
Frazer, Dr. Kenneth, 63
Free Assembly, 14
Free Speech, 14, 100, 104
Free Trade, 51, 60, 90

General Warrant, 98
George, Lloyd, 86
German Supreme Council, 27
Germany, 14, 19 n., 20, 25 n., 29, 37, 39–41, 53–55, 72, 92, 104, 120, 122
Glamorgan, 94
Gradualism, 28, 80 ff.
Great War, 40, 64
Greater Britain, 120

Harbell, G. S., 50
Hayek, F. von, 78
Heines, 37
Hemingway, Ernest, 124
Henri, Ernst, 33
Hindenburg, 105
Hitler, 13, 15, 29, 32, 34, 36, 37, 72, 105, 122
Home Secretary, 94
Horne, Sir Robert, 49
Horridge, Mr. Justice, 102
House of Commons, 46, 55, 58, 63, 91, 97, 135
House of Lords, 121, 133, 135
Houston, Lady, 132
Hunger Marchers, 97
Hyde Park, 14

INDEX 139

Imperial Chemical Industries, 56
Imperial Communications Company, 80
Imperial Defence, 58
Imperial Fascist League, 117
Imperial Smelting Corporation, 49
Imperialism, 22–27, 57, 130
Import Duties, 24, 53
Incitement to Disaffection Act, 14, 96
Income Tax, 70
Independent Labour Party, 117
India, 41, 49, 52, 112, 116, 121, 132
Industrial Revolution, 75
Inflation, 30
Inskip, Sir Thomas, 71, 97, 98, 100, 101
International Army, 26
International Labour Office, 54
International Police Force, 26
International Tin Committee, 49
International Zinc Cartel, 49
Irish Free State, 54
Italy, 14, 29, 34, 39, 40, 73, 92, 104, 120

January Club, 132
Japan, 26, 41, 55, 57, 58, 111
Japanese Chamber of Commerce, 26
Japanese Economic League, 26
Junkers, 37

Keynes, J. M., 52

King George, 88–89
Krupp, von Bohlen, 36, 38

Labour Exchange, 95, 129
Labour Party, 28, 79 ff., 84, 96, 113, 114, 118, 127, 132
Labour Research, 64 n., 107
Laissez-faire, 33, 61, 76
Laski, H. T., 76 n., 102
League of Nations, 26, 46
Liberalism, 25
Lloyd, Lord, 116, 132
London County Council, 133
London Passenger Transport Act, 80
Ludendorff, 14

MacDonald, G. R., 40, 55, 58, 62, 69, 88, 96 n., 102, 105
Macmillan Report, 42, 45
Malnutrition, 63 ff.
Managers, 129
Manchuria, 58
Marxian Socialism, 78
May, Sir George, 81
Means Test, 62, 70, 84
Medical Officer, 62
Mexico, 42
Minister of Health, 63, 65
Ministry of Labour, 69
Mises, von, 76
Mond, Sir Alfred, 80
Monopoly, 23, 24, 32, 34, 59, 60, 129, 130
Mosley, Sir Oswald, 13, 116–120, 136
Morrison, Herbert, 80, 126
Mosley Memorandum, 119
Mowrer, E., 33 n.
Multiple Shops, 128

Municipal Reformers, 71
Mussolini, 13, 29, 32, 34, 59, 73, 105
Mutiny Act, 98

National Citizens' Guild, 71
National Debt, 41, 88
National Labour Committee, 69
National Self-sufficiency, 24-25, 66, 72
National Shipbuilders' Security, Ltd., 48
National Unemployed Workers' Movement, 102
Nationalization, 32, 38, 115
Naval Disarmament Conference, 58
Near East, 40
New Party, 119, 120
New Statesman and Nation, 48, 94, 98
New Zealand, 54, 108
Nordwestgrupper der Essen und Stahlindustrie, 33
Norway, 54

Official Secrets Act, 98
Olympia, 14, 93, 131
Oppenheim, E. Phillips, 95
Organization for Maintenance of Supplies, 92
Orlando, Signor, 15
Ottawa Conference, 52, 54, 112

Pacifism, 100
Papen, Von, 36, 37
Parliamentary Government, 14, 28, 40, 76, 83 ff.
Parmoor, Lord, 99

Percy, Lord Eustace, 20
Planning, 24-25, 129
Police Bill, 93
Police Federation, 93
Polish Corridor, 35
Political Democracy, 21, 22, 28, 29, 32, 39, 75, 83 ff., 104, 114, 115
Poor Law, 62, 69
Post Office Savings, 88
Post Office Workers, 127
Press, 58, 72, 91
Private Army, 30, 94, 115, 117, 120, 131
Proctor, Major, 96
Professional Men, 129, 130
Profit Sharing, 80

Quotas, 24, 66, 110

Rationalization, 34, 46, 80, 106
Reg. *v.* Eagleton, 101
Reichswehr, 37
Rhine, as British Frontier, 59
Ricardo, 76
Roehm, 37
Rogers, Lindsay, 90
Rothermere, Lord, 71, 116, 123, 131
Royal Commission on Unemployment Insurance, 44
Royal Defence Corps, 95
Ruhr Steel Trust, 33
Russia, 76

Saturday Review, 132
Schleicher, 37
Scottish Fascist Democratic Party, 118
Seinosuké Go, Baron, 26

INDEX 141

Shacht, Dr., 38
Shop Assistants, 128
Simon, Leo John, 56
Singapore, 58
"Small Men," 30, 35, 72, 128–130
Smith, F. E., 116
Social Democracy, 28, 31, 35
Social Murder, 65
Socialism, 32, 90, 100, 114, 128, 133, 135
Socialist League, 114, 133
Society of Friends, 99
Stahlhelm, 36
Statist, 49, 50
Storm Troops, 36, 37
Strachey, John, 51, 52, 119
Strasser, Gregor, 32
Students, 30
Subsidies, 24, 54, 66
Surtaxes, 24
Sweden, 54

Tariffs, 24, 52–55, 59, 60, 72, 90, 107, 108, 110, 113, 132
Tawney, R. H., 67
Teachers, 127
Technicians, 30, 129–130
Times, The, 49–50, 80
Times Trade Supplement, 45
Third International, 96
Thomas, J. H., 118
Thyssen, 38
Trade Unions, 28, 32, 60, 61, 113–115, 126–128, 134–135

Trades Union Act, 92
Training Camps, 69–70
Transitional Benefit, 62
Treasury, 119
Trenchard, Lord, 102

Ulster, 115
Unemployment, 16, 17, 19, 20, 28, 30, 34, 41–46, 62, 63, 65, 118, 127, 132
Unemployment Act (1934), 14, 62, 70, 72
Unemployment Assistance Board, 70
Unemployment Insurance, 34, 62, 81
United Empire Fascist Party, 117
United States of America, 17, 26, 41, 49, 53, 55, 57–58, 90, 111

Versailles, Treaty of, 15, 17
Vickers, Ltd., 97

West Indies, 108
Wilkes, John, 101, 102
William Beardmore & Co., 48
Woolcombers' Mutual Association, Ltd., 49
World Economic Conference, 24

Zaharoff, Sir Basil, 25

For Product Safety Concerns and Information please contact our EU representative GPSR@taylorandfrancis.com
Taylor & Francis Verlag GmbH, Kaufingerstraße 24, 80331 München, Germany

www.ingramcontent.com/pod-product-compliance
Lightning Source LLC
Chambersburg PA
CBHW061416300426
44114CB00015B/1963